Post-Adjustment Theories:
A Few Research Trails for
African Economies

State of the Literature Series

Les théories du post-ajustment: quelques pistes de recherche pour les économies africaines (1-1998)

Hakim Ben Hammouda

Du gouvernement privé indirect (1-1999)

Achille Mbembe

Science politique réflexive et savoirs sur les pratiques politiques en Afrique noire (2-1999)

Luc Sindjoun

On private indirect government (1-2000)

Achille Mbembe

Post-Adjustment Theories: A Few Research Trails for African Economies

Hakim Ben Hammouda

State of the Literature Series

No. 2 - 2000

Post-Adjustment Theories: A Few Research Trails for

African Economies

State of the Literature Series 2/2000

© Council for the Development of Social Science Research in Africa 2000

Translated from the French **Les théories du post-ajustment: quelques pistes de recherche pour les économies africaines**

© Council for the Development of Social Science Research in Africa 1998

Avenue Cheikh Anta Diop, BP 3304, Dakar, Senegal

ISSN 0851-0466

Typesetting by Djibril Fall

Printed by CODESRIA

CODESRIA would like to express its gratitude to the Swedish Agency for International Development Cooperation Agency (SIDA/SAREC), the International Development Research Centre (IDRC), the Ford Foundation, the MacArthur Foundation, the Carnegie Corporation, the Norwegian Ministry of Foreign Affairs, the Danish Agency for International Development (DANIDA) the French Ministry of Cooperation, the United Nations Development Programme, the Netherlands Ministry of Foreign Affairs, the Rockefeller Foundation, and the Government of Senegal for their support of its research, training and publications programmes.

Contents

The Author

Hakim Ben Hammouda holds a Ph.D in international economics and has held various teaching positions in universities in France and Burundi. Among his numerous publications include *Les pensées ethiques en économies* (Paris: Harmattan, 1997); *Le Maghreb: enlisement ou nouveau départ?*, coauthored, (Paris Harmattan, 1996); *Tunisie: ajustement et difficulté de l'insertion internationale,* (Paris Harmattan, 1995); *Afrique-Monde arabe: Echec de l'insertion internationale,* coauthored (Paris: Harmattan, 1995); *Burundi: L'histoire économique et politique d'un conflit* (Paris: Harmattan, 1994). He is currently the Senior Progamme Officer, Training, Grants and Outreach, CODESRIA.

Introduction

The Council for the Development of Social Science Research in Africa (CODESRIA) has been an active participant in the broad movement of critical reaction to the results of SAPs in Africa. CODESRIA has organised a series of activities dealing with the subject. Among them, the following conferences should be noted:

- "The adjustment of African economies to the crisis", 1985;
- "The social impact of the economic crisis and African reactions to it ", 1986;
- "Adjustment, de-industrialisation and the urban African crisis", 1987;
- "Structural adjustment policies in Africa", 1991;
- "The South Commission and Africa in the 1990s", 1993;
- "Crises, conflicts and change: responses and perspectives", 1995.

These various activities have produced a considerable literature on the results of African experience of adjustment (Fall 1997; Tshibaka 1998; Mkandawire et al. 1995).

These conferences and critical analyses on the effects of adjustment in Africa led to the formation of a multinational research group on "African Perspectives on Structural Adjustment Programmes". This group has undertaken a systematic analysis of structural adjustment programmes in Africa, in order to make a full assessment of the reform movement, both at national and continental levels.[1]

---

[1] The findings of the working group have just been published. The first volume is, *Our Continent, Our Future,* edited by Thandika Mkandawire and Charles Soludo, CODESRIA/IDRC/AWP: Dakar, Ottawa, New Jersey, 1999. The second volume, a collection of fourteen background papers, *African Voices on Structural Adjustment* by the same editors is in press.

The aim of the present paper is to combine the critical reaction to structural adjustment, which has been going on for more than a decade at CODESRIA, with the new approaches of a number of schools of thought that seek to go further than the Washington consensus.

At the end of the 1980s and in throughout the 1990s, the field of development economics underwent far-reaching changes. The failure of attempts at structural adjustment in most developing countries challenged the theoretical foundations and the proposals for development of the Washington consensus.

Development theory steered progressively away from the strict model of general equilibrium, which had dominated thought and practice in development throughout the 1980s. Consequently, a new theory of development economics, which can be described as post-adjustment development economics, took the place of the Washington consensus. This new development economics includes all those theoretical approaches that diverge from the Walrassian model, by recognising the imperfections of the market and the inability of orthodox stabilisation and adjustment policies, which are inspired by this basic model, to bring about the changes that are necessary for a return to sustained growth in the developing countries. Development theory could thus not go on remaining indifferent to the social problems of the people of the South, which were the result of the stabilisation programmes and the weakness of growth produced by the reforms. These trends sounded the death knell of the triumphant liberalism of the 1980s, and led to the development of a new era, concerned with rebuilding the "empire of chaos" (Amin 1991), which took over from the neo-liberal obsession in the early 1980s with destroying the old order.

The renewal of development theory was also influenced by new trends in economic theory and the decline of rational anticipation theories in favour of a new synthesis of different theoretical approaches and schools (Hammouda 1997). Indeed, neo-classical theory progressively abandoned the basic Walrassian model, developed a methodological neo-classicism, which recognised the place and role of contractual procedures in regulating societies, and attempted to integrate them into its analysis. Along with its abandonment of the normative character of the basic model and an increasingly keen desire to test its relevancy, the neo-classical movement confirmed its methodological preference for microeconomics and for the importance of analysing inter-individual relationships between actors. At the same time, it could be observed that the principal rivals of the neo-classical movement had abandoned holistic methods and sought to discover the contributions of methodological individualism to heterodox analyses. This evolution brought the heterodox movements closer to the neo-classical movement. Certain authors even referred to a new synthesis (Abraham-Frois 1993). The synthesis influenced work on development economics, and is responsible for the continuing changes in the field of economic analysis.

Post adjustment development economics includes a number of theoretical movements and approaches. While these different movements may agree on the failure of the strict model of general equilibrium in the field of development, they are, however, far from sharing the same analysis of the causes of this failure and the perspectives for research that are open to development economics. According to some scholars, the crisis affecting development economics and in particular the Washington consensus is due to its normativeness from an epistemological standpoint. The neo-classical movement advanced the hypothesis that unrestrained competition and interaction between the plans of different economic operators would ensure the regulation of the market system. Consequently, this movement could not grasp and understand the imperfections of the market and its inability by itself to ensure the socialisation of individuals in a decentralised society. This analysis led to the development of new theoretical approaches that were stimulated by the research in progress. More precisely, it would attempt to break away from the normative nature of the basic model and increase its ability to explain, in particular by modifying the basic hypotheses (Bardhan 1993).

According to other writers, the failure of structural adjustment was not merely the failure of a specific movement in development economics, but also the bankruptcy of a project to Westernise the world that had formed the basis for this policy. According to this cultural approach, the West had used development economics to impose its own blueprint of society on the different countries of the South. The West's universalist claims led it to destroy traditional communities and grassroots solidarity. By its development of trade relationships, the West had imposed its model of social organisation and political modernity, which was based on the individual becoming independent from the community and on the introduction of specific forms of political and economic rationalisation. From this point of view, the crisis of the Washington consensus was only a further sign of how impossible it was to transpose the standards of Western culture and civilisation onto other worlds, and should induce the North to reconsider its universalist positions and to adopt more relativistic attitudes, which were more in keeping with the principle of the right to be different.

Four main approaches can be discerned in the move to renew development theory in the post-adjustment period:

- the first seeks to look for new inspiration by returning to the work of forerunners in the field, such as Hirschman, with his unbalanced growth, or Rosenstein-Rodan with the Big Push theory. This approach has also been influenced by the theoretical findings of work on endogenous growth (Krugman 1993),

- the second approach to development problems concentrates on elements linked to market imperfection, and to the place and role of institutions in co-ordinating the activities of the different economic operators. This approach challenges the ability of any auction system to ensure the convergence of the contradictory interests of different economic operators and gives more importance to the different institutions that play a role in the regulation and running of decentralised economies (Antonelli and Raimondo 1992; Guillaumont 1995),

- the third approach involves the renewal of the structuralist approach, which has been able to use criticism of the orthodox approach to stabilisation, in order to make a new and heterodox presentation of development problems,

- The fourth approach takes the opposite tack from the three preceding ones. It regards the crisis of the Washington consensus as a proof of the failure of development economics. This approach calls for an end of the attempt to Westernise the world, which has been undertaken since the end of colonisation by the North.

The present paper attempts to study the rise of post-adjustment development economics through a critical presentation of the different approaches, which have changed the analysis of underdeveloped economies. However, despite these changes, we shall advance the hypothesis that these different schools of thought have been unable to overcome the crisis in development economics. From a theoretical viewpoint, the recent changes have not provided economists with the theoretical tools and grids they need to analyse the transformations and transitions in the developing world since the end of the 1980s. Different analyses in recent years have stressed the breakdown of the unity of the developing world and the different routes followed by national economies. The evolution of developing countries from the mid-1980s on is different from their course in the 1960s and 1970s. During the first few decades of independence, developing countries undertook large-scale economic and social modernisation programmes. This effort enabled them to organise relatively strong economic growth dynamics, and to form a united group at the international level, in order to negotiate better integration into the international economy. However, with the debt crisis and depression of the 1980s, the context changed completely. Deflationary problems extended to underdeveloped economies, breaking the unity of the developing world in the process. Some countries, such as those in Southeast Asia, were able to maintain their growth rates and pursue their efforts to build competitive national economies. Other countries, such as the majority of African countries, have declined into marginalisation and chaos. Finally, other countries, such as those in Latin America, maintained with difficulty a status-quo position in the international economy, without managing to establish a more dynamic participation (Toye 1987). *Thus, the multiplicity of transitions currently seems to be the fundamental characteristic of the accumulation of capital in the Third World. However, the new approaches to development economics do not enable us to understand and analyse the changes in progress in all underdeveloped economies.*

Furthermore, since the failure of attempts to modernise, based on the nation-state, developing countries have been torn between the option of globalisation and international integration, and the temptation to turn inwards and to cut themselves off from the world. *From this point of view as well, the new analyses of development have not been able to formulate new strategies to help underdeveloped countries to manage change.*

The two limitations to the different schools of post-adjustment development economics, which we have just described, are due to their static conception of development. *From this standpoint, we put forward the hypothesis that the principal schools of post-adjustment development economics do not have a dynamic conception of the realities of underdeveloped countries, and thus they cannot understand and even less explain the diversity of changes in the South.* Certainly, most scholars have taken an interest in the recent changes in the developing world. But it seems to us that most of their analyses do not go beyond the level of empirical observation and are unable to explain the evolutions and changes that are going on.

In the present paper, we shall attempt to examine the different approaches to post-adjustment development economics. The first part of this paper focuses on recent economic debates that have influenced current trends in development theory. The second part examines the schools of thought which, following P. Krugman's analyses and research on endogenous growth, have sought to renew recent conceptions of development economics by returning to the work of the pioneers. In the third part, we examine recent work by the institutionalist and conventionalist approaches. Part four will be devoted to the new structuralist and Keynesian approaches. The last part will deal with the cultural approach.

Section I

The 1990s: A new context in the field of economics

The strict Walrassian model depends on the two basic principles of perfect competition and the rationality of economic actors . In a world governed by these two principles, consumers and producers meet in the market place and exchange goods and services. They respect the rules of market operations and the creation of an equilibrium. This equilibrium is established in all markets, and the economy as a whole can be seen as a system of interdependent markets in a position of equilibrium.

The basic Walrassian model thus regards the economy as a space which is by definition free from conflict, and in which operators have access to complete information in order to make their plans. This basic model describes a "virtual" universe characterised by perfect competition, an atomicity of participants, a homogeneity of products and free entry into the markets. As P. Cahuc notes, "It is a market with a very large number of buyers and sellers, all fully informed but not acting in concert, exchanging exactly similar goods, at prices that are determined by the market itself" (Cahuc 1993).

This model can be strongly criticised for its lack of realism and its normative content. Increasing criticism at the beginning of the 1980s led neoclassical economists to adapt their work, with a view to improving the relevancy and explanatory power of the Walrassian model. This adaptation of pure theory was essentially constructed around three themes:

- challenging the exogenous nature of growth in traditional models and seeking endogenous factors of growth,

- abandoning the hypotheses of perfect competition and complete information in the model of general equilibrium, and developing research on market imperfections,

- a further look at the role of institutions and conventions in co-ordinating the plans of different economic operators in a decentralised economy.

Heterodox thinkers echoed these new themes of study in the new microeconomics. From a microeconomic standpoint, the neo-Keynesians were increasingly concerned with market imperfections linked to price rigidities. Furthermore, regulation theories reviewed by conventionalists increasingly sought to understand economic situations that diverged from the pure and perfect competitive market. These shared concerns among the three approaches to economic theory have developed into a research programme that has exercised a wide influence on post-adjustment development economics. Its major themes have been market imperfections, the limited rationality of actors and the place of institutions in the regulation of the economic system.

The nature and factors of growth

A new view of traditional economic growth theories began to be taken in the mid-1980s, with the emergence of endogenous growth theories (Amable and Guellec 1992, Artus 1993, Henin and Ralle 1994, Lordon 1991). Contrary to traditional conceptions that analysed economic growth as the product of an increase in the working population and exogenous increases in productivity, these new approaches took into account the endogenous character of the process of economic growth. According to these theories, the explanation of growth should not be limited to increases in the factors of production, but should take other aspects into consideration, such as the quality of human capital, increasing returns, and the importance of internal learning processes and endogenous technical progress. This theoretical reconsideration had consequences for traditional recommendations in terms of economic policy and more particularly on the hypothesis, championed by the new classical macroeconomics, of the ineffectiveness of government action on economic regulation.

Since their emergence, endogenous growth theories have examined the principal factors explaining growth dynamics and their self-sustaining characteristics. In keeping with this, the first model of endogenous growth, formulated by P. Romer, stressed the importance of investment in the economic growth process (Romer 1986).

P. Romer modified the hypothesis of constant returns of scale, but located them outside the firm, in order to maintain the context of pure and perfect competition. In more recent work, P. Romer examined the role of technological innovation and of spending on research and development in economic growth (Romer 1990). In this model, P. Romer put forward a multiple-sector economy, in which capital is not homogeneous but belongs to different generations of inputs. In this context, new inputs, manufactured with increased returns, make it possible to improve the productivity of the end goods sector and to increase the general efficiency of the economy.

R. Lucas gives special weight to the accumulation of human capital by individuals as an explanation of endogenous growth (Lucas 1988). The issue was also examined by G. Becker, K. M. Murphy and R. Tamura, who looked again at population growth, which according to Solow, was an exogenous source of economic growth. They considered that it was in the best interest of economies to restrict population growth, so as to ensure a better standard of human capital that was more able to support a process of sustainable growth (Becker, Murphy et al. 1990).

Other models of endogenous growth have studied the importance of public infrastructures in the growth process (Barro 1990, 1991; Barro and Martin 1992). According to these authors, these public assets make it possible to improve the productivity of private agents and increase the process of growth.

Theories of endogenous growth thus break with traditional conceptions and see economic growth as a self-sustaining process, which may be influenced by increasing returns and various types of externalities, such as technological innovation, know-how or public assets.

Market imperfections

The hypothesis of pure and perfect competition holds a central position in the pure model of general equilibrium. This hypothesis has been abandoned by the new microeconomics in order to increase the relevancy of the basic model. W. J. Baumol thus challenges free entry to the market with the theory of contestable markets (Baumol et al. 1988, 1991). According to this line of thinking, a contestable market is defined as one

that can be entered or left without incurring any costs. According to W. Baumol, this concept is a better reflection of the monopoly that exists in certain areas and is an extension of pure and perfect competition. According to Baumol, contestable markets are beneficial for national economies and businesses, to the extent that they ensure:

- non-excessive prices,
- limited waste,
- elimination of subsidies,
- optimal pricing.

W.Baumol recognises, however, that the scope for contestable markets is currently limited. Because of this, businesses are only interested in actual competition within their fields, and do not worry about potential competition that could come from the entry of new firms into the market. This situation enables businesses to implement sub-optimal pricing and obtain quasi-monopoly profits.

The issue of operators' information is also at the heart of the argument about market imperfections. This has led to the development of a movement known as information economics, whose aim is to study the rational behaviour of economic operators facing difficulties in obtaining information on products. This new discipline deals with the study of strategic interactions between economic operators with asymmetrical access to information.

Akerlof's research on the dependency of prices on the quality of goods was the foundation of information economics (Akerlof 1970). In his article, A. G. Akerlof studied the used-car market and formed the hypothesis that sellers had information on the quality of the cars, while buyers only had expectations. In that context, buyers refused to pay high prices because they knew there were lemons on the market. At such a price, however, sellers only sell lemons and withdraw good quality cars. This is a case of *adverse selection,* in which good quality products are driven off the market. This phenomenon can lead to a reduction of trade or even to a market collapse, if agents believe that only poorquality goods are placed on the market.

Akerlof's groundbreaking article led to a proliferation of research demonstrating that the freedom of operators in the market can lead to the disappearance of quality products, and recommending the establishment of procedures to reveal the quality of products or to ensure recourse against poorquality goods (Stiglitz 1987; Belloc 1987; Orléan 1991).

In addition to adverse selection, information economics has studied the problem of *moral risk or moral hazard,* related to the fact that a certain number of operators can reduce the amount of risk they take in trading, by actions that cannot be observed by other operators . In moral hazard situations, incentive procedures should be established, so that operators with private information act in an optimal manner for those who do not have such information, while in adverse selection situations, incentives should enable economic operators to obtain information on the quality of goods. Thus, means and procedures need to be established in moral hazard situations, to ensure an equal sharing of risks by traders (Laffont 1987).

Moral hazard is generally apprehended through *principal-agent* models in which the principal performs an action for an agent or representative, against payment. This action may take the form of production in relationships between employers and employees, harvests in relationships between landowners and farmers, or court decisions in relationships between clients and lawyers. This type of contract poses difficulties when an agent's action is not perfectly transparent, and is consequently difficult for the principal to assess. In such cases, both parties must define a mini-institution enabling them to share the risks and encourage the agent to act in the best interests of the principal.

New microeconomics work on market imperfection was followed by neo-Keynesian work. The neo-Keynesians postulate an economic universe characterised by four basic hypotheses. First, that the behaviour of economic operators is rational and obeys the principle of optimisation under constraint. Furthermore, markets are imperfect and do not follow

14

the rules of pure and perfect competition. Information is incomplete, which means that information cannot be acquired without cost. Finally, markets are incomplete, i.e. there are procedures or contracts extraneous to the market that govern relationships between economic operators .

Within that universe, the best-known model is that of R. J. Gordon, who examines the elasticity of prices. This model is used by Gordon to study the evolution of price elasticity in various economies over the 1873-1987 period. The study showed that in the American economy, price elasticity remained constant between 1954 and 1987, and between 1873 and 1914. With some nuances, Gordon's findings for the other economies he studied (United Kingdom, Japan, France and Germany) were quite similar (Gordon 1990). This research shows that the elasticity of prices was no greater during the Great Depression than it was during the three decades of prosperity following World War II. From a theoretical standpoint, this means that price adjustments were common, but that their impact on the markets was not immediate.

Against this background, the neo-Keynesians have taken an interest in the reasons for low elasticity and the nature of the price rigidities that caused them. However, before introducing rigidities, the neo-Keynesians formed the hypothesis that firms are price-makers, which differentiates them from the Walrassian universe in which they are price-takers. If they are price-makers, then firms can rationally refuse to change prices, despite information received from the market. This behaviour leads to rigidities, which make price adjustment sticky. At this level, there is a distinction to be made between nominal rigidity and real rigidity (Romer 1993). Rigidity is said to be nominal when an operator's behaviour does not promote flexibility in the price of a good, but has no impact on the price of other goods. Rigidity is real, however, when the relative pricing system is disturbed.

15

Neo- Keynesians argue that nominal rigidities are the result of imperfect competition in the market, which may encourage firms in a monopoly position to fix prices. Parallel to this explanation, the neo-Keynesians also refer to the menu costs hypothesis to explain price stickiness (Mankiw 1985). Thus, a firm can refuse to change its prices, despite variations in demand, if the material costs of changing prices are high and the image of its product can be affected.

Real rigidities may stem from the mark-up method used by businesses to calculate their costs. According to this method, sales prices are calculated by increasing the average cost by a fixed amount known as a mark-up. In such a case, if the average cost covers payment of labour input and intermediary products, the mark-up represents capital costs and profits. This method of calculation is a major source of real rigidity, since it makes it possible to avoid sales price increases aimed at maximising profits. Furthermore, it enables firms to disclaim responsibility for price changes.

A. Okun's distinction between auction-type markets and clientele markets provides another explanation for real rigidities (Okun 1981). In auction-type markets, operators alter prices whenever demand changes. However, in clientele markets, relationships between economic operators are governed by an implicit contract, so that businesses fix their prices and undertake to guarantee their stability and the quality of their products.

These rigidities led the neo-Keynesians to form the hypothesis of near rationality, which is slightly different from the traditional hypothesis of rationality, since it does not involve perfect price flexibility. Under these conditions, equilibrium is generally below optimum, compared with the Walrassian equilibrium (Akerlof and Yellen 1985).

In addition to the study of price rigidities in markets for goods, the neo-Keynesians have also shown an interest in studying the labour market. In their analyses of the labour market, they rework the traditional framework with the hypothesis of rational operators. . This allowed for adjustment between labour supply and demand through flexibility in real wages. Beyond a certain natural unemployment rate, unemployment was said to be voluntary. However, this proposition is refuted by the neo-Keynesians, who demonstrate that rigidities in real wages block labour market adjustments and are therefore responsible for involuntary unemployment. The contribution of the neo-Keynesians at this level, particularly through implicit contract and efficiency wage theories, has been to demonstrate that rigidities are the result of rational behaviour by economic operators.

Institutions and conventions at the heart of co-ordination

In addition to market imperfections, recent work in economic theory has examined the different institutions that play an important role in co-ordinating the actions of different operators and regulating the decentralised economic system. The Hobbesian criticism of liberal society makes it necessary to consider institutions, together with the difficulties in the co-ordination among operators in situations of strategic interaction and in the absence of any central authority (Villé 1990). Indeed, in an individualistic society, guided by profit maximisation, operators might defraud and cheat, so as to serve their interests more effectively. Such an approach could lead to social disorder and breakdown. To ensure the coherent functioning of society, Hobbes proposed the introduction of a supra-individual authority, Leviathan, to which individuals would give up part of their prerogatives in order to ensure the preservation of the whole . These philosophical and economic reflections prompted the new microeconomics to introduce institutions into their analysis of decentralised economies.

Considering institutions and agreements is not a new approach in microeconomic theory (*Economie appliquée* 1990; Brousseau 1993). As early as 1987, R. Coase diverged from the basic model by considering the firm as a locus of co-ordination outside the market (Coase 1987). This school of thought , known as neo-institutionalism, has extended in recent years to examine the complementarity between organisations and markets (Alchian and Demsetz 1972; Williamson 1975, 1985). In addition, D. North sought to explain historical phenomena by taking into account the knowledge gained through the neo-institutional approach (North and Thomas 1973; North 1990). While their studies recognise the importance of institutions in the running of decentralised economies, however, the neo- institutionalists follow the neoclassical line in holding that institutions are a result of rational choices by operators (Guerrien 1990).

R. H. Coase's transaction cost theory has an important place in the neo-institutional line of thought (Gillis 1987). In his work, Coase sought to understand the reasons that motivated firms to develop their own internal organisation and avoid recourse to the market. According to transaction theory, this internalisation can be explained by the cost of outsourcing, especially when the market is imperfect. In this way, a firm can save on market costs, and a boundary is established between it and the market. Relationships between internalisation and the market are governed by the principle of marginal costs. This theory has long been criticised and has been accused of being descriptive and lacking an operational definition of transaction costs.

Despite this criticism, however, Coase's analysis is still influential in the field of political economy. For instance, K. Arrow takes up Coase's

18

thinking when he argues that the firm and the market are alternative forms of economic organisation (Arrow 1974). S. Hymer also uses Coase's analyses in his study of direct foreign investments (Hymer 1976). In his research, S. Hymer explains that the development of multinationals is linked to the imperfection of international markets and firms' desire to internalise their activities in order to reduce risks. Finally, O. Williamson extends Coase's research by developing organisation theory, which uses a neoclassical framework to analyse forms of co-ordination outside the market as vertical integration processes within firms (Williamson 1975, 1985).

In the end, by setting aside the limitations of the hypothesis of the auctioneer, the new microeconomics is able to study a world much richer than the Walrassian world . Despite its increased relevancy, however, the new microeconomics is obliged to accept the market's inability to explain the phenomenon of socialisation in its entirety. Hence, its recognition of the importance of standards and institutions in regulating decentralised economies.

These concerns are also shared by the French "conventionalists". Convention theory is a new approach that developed in France in the 1980s. The research is motivated by the difficulties of the neoclassical framework in understanding economic situations that diverge from the pure and perfect competitive market. However, the goal of the economists adhering to this movement is not to correct and extend the framework of standard theory (Dupuy et al. 1989). Instead, as A. Orléan explains, it is "a collective work under way for some time, which focuses on analysing capitalist economies, and which recognises the essential role played by non-market forms of co-ordination, production and resource allocation" (Orléan 1994:13).

The development of this school of thought meets a series of methodological and theoretical requirements. The first lies in the development of a multidisciplinary approach combining economics with sociology, in order to analyse various forms of joint action and co-ordination. The second concern of the conventionalists is to go beyond what they view as the sterile opposition between orthodoxy and heterodoxy in the field of political economy. This presupposes that convention theory must take account of the contributions of extended standard theory to the study of organisational and institutional phenomena and must recognise the importance of methodological individualism. Opposition is outdated and it is time to draw closer or even for a synthesis, since, as Orléan writes, "there is now a pervasive feeling of belonging to the same scientific community faced with difficult problems" (Orléan 1994:15).

Despite this common will to develop a broad eclectic framework, which would provide for a broad gathering of non-orthodox approaches, different conceptions of conventions exist among economists. According to one view, a convention can be defined as "a mechanism constituting an agreement of wills, like its product, having a mandatory normative force... and should be understood both as the result of individual actions and as a framework that constrains its subjects" (Dupuy et al. 1989). This relatively abstract definition is set out more precisely by followers of convention theory in specific fields of analysis. For instance, R. Salais uses the notion to study labour relations. The point of departure of his analysis is the neoclassical model's inability to account for labour relations, since they are established between employers and employees before work is carried out (Salais 1989). Indeed, according to Salais, labour relations depend on two principles: the making of a contract when labour is hired and the carrying out of labour in production. These two principles correspond to two logical equivalencies: an equivalency between wages and the future length of work , and an equivalency between the actual working time and the goods produced. According to R. Salais, this ambivalence in labour relations gives rise to uncertainties over the production and the quality of goods. This uncertainty is permanently eliminated from the real economy, according to Salais, by the establishment of two conventions:

- a "productivity" convention, that makes it possible to replace non-existent labour with an alternative standard at the time of exchange;

- an "unemployment convention", which constitutes an procedure for the evaluation after the event of the productivity convention and allows employers to make adjustments between forecasts and actual production.

On this basis, R. Salais defines labour relations "as a compromise, which generates tension, between two equivalency principles, one which, when a bargain is struck between an employer and an employee, establishes an equivalence between future working time and wages, and one that, creates an equivalence, in the subsequent course of production, between the actual working time and the goods produced" (Salais 1989:237).

Uncertainty arising from the de-structuring of growth dynamics in capitalist economies in the current crisis is also a factor in A. Orléan's ideas on conventions. He argues that uncertainty is a manifestation of the inability of the Walrassian market to ensure the co-ordination of individual actions in a decentralised economy (Orléan 1991). Even though neoclassical theory recognises uncertainty, it reduces it, according to A. Orléan, to a calculable risk, which makes it unable to explain the evolution of modern economies. According to Orléan, uncertainty should mean that economists accept the idea of new elements appearing that

21

cannot be incorporated into previous data. This uncertainty creates situations where there is a general lack of confidence in the constraints of the social order (Orléan 1989).

This widespread lack of confidence can lead to generalised risks for socio-economic organisational systems, which cannot be overcome by agreements or private assurances. Conventions are, therefore, a necessity, and their legitimacy, according to A. Orléan "stems from the specific existence of co-ordination imposed on the social system by uncertainty, i.e. a widespread withdrawal from arrangements" (Orléan 1989:244). The author gives two examples of this type of convention: lenders of last resort and savings insurance. However, more than studying individual forms of co-ordination, convention theory should make it possible "to understand how collective reasoning is constituted and what resources need to be mobilised to establish it" (Orléan 1994:16). Convention theory economists should "have access to formal tools enabling them to understand the interrelations of various market, organisational, institutional or ethical resources and how their interrelations can be made coherent despite the apparent diversity of the reasoning behind them" (Orléan 1994:16).

This search for general co-ordination mechanisms can also be found in the work of O. Favereau. His analysis of conventions is founded on a criticism of standard theory, which reduces the rationality of individual behaviour to the optimisation and co-ordination of individual behaviour towards market regulation (Favereau 1989). Furthermore, extended standard theory, which includes such approaches as transaction theory, and incentive, agency and contract models, reduces non-market forms of co-ordination to individual agreements between agents. However, the relevance of the basic model can only be enhanced at the expense of a certain loss of general coherence. From this point of view, , the advantage of convention theory, according to O. Favereau, resides in the fact that it attempts to account for the existence of "collective cognitive mechanisms", in addition to individual contracts and rules, which are capable of ensuring the coherence of individual decisions in a decentralised economy (Favereau 1989). By taking these conventions into account, O. Favereau is able to give an alternative presentation of the decentralised economy, conceived as a population of organisations (in the sense of internal markets), structured by the play of reproduction and coherence.

The elements presented in these different conceptions of convention theory help us come to grips with the principal characteristics of this new theoretical approach. The theory is born of criticism of the Walrassian model that reduces co-ordination between economic operators to market regulation - hence its claim to heterodoxy. Furthermore, the theory is not satisfied by the extended standard theory's adjustments to the basic model, since consideration of non-market forms of co-ordination remains limited to individual contracts and agreements. From this viewpoint, convention theory aims to provide an alternative approach, by establishing conventions arising from collective behaviour by economic operators as a regulating principle in decentralised economies.

Despite these statements of principle, it should, however, be noted that convention theory comes back in concrete analysis to extended standard theory.. This connection forms the foundation for a new broad synthesis that conventionalists strongly favour, hoping to get beyond the sterile opposition between orthodoxy and heterodoxy. This connection is immediately apparent in methodological choices, including the abandonment of holistic approaches and the choice of individualism, despite the claims of conventionalists on the necessity of maintaining a global approach to economics.

This concordance between the two lines of thinking is also visible in the conventionalists' use of the theory of uncooperative game theory to analyse interactions between economic operators. Although this theory enables us to abandon the auctioneer hypothesis of the traditional model, it has difficulty in explaining the viability of decentralised economies. Finally, the link between the two theories can also be observed in their conceptions of institutions. On this level, despite a reference to J. R. Commons, one of the founding fathers of American institutionalism in the 1920s and 1930s, the conventionalists seem much closer to the vision of the new American institutional economics. While this new institutional economics styles itself as a descendant of American institutionalism, the two movements seem to have diverged over a number of issues (Dutraive 1993). The difference between the old and new American institutional approaches lies in their conception of institutions. While an institution, according to Commons, provides a series of rules and standards to which operators can conform, in the view of the new institutional economics, institutions are reduced to the forms of co-ordination generated by market imperfections. Furthermore, institutionalism recognises and seeks to integrate the action of structures in the definition of co-ordination institutions, whereas the new institutional economics restricts its study of institutions to individual arrangements and agreements. This opposition stems from the methodological opposition in the two approaches between holism and individualism..

In summary , recent research in economic theory has led to a broad and eclectic synthesis of heterodox approaches, such as conventionalism, the new Walrassian microeconomics and the neo- Keynesians. This evolution has come about through an abandonment of holistic methodological positions and the rejection of the idea of constructing an alternative hypothesis to general equilibrium in the case of Keynesians and heterodox theories, and the aim of the new microeconomics to develop a grid to explain the functioning of economies. This convergence has made it possible to outline a new research programme in the field of economics, focusing on the study of market imperfections and aiming to improve analysis of co-ordination phenomena between economic operators in decentralised economies. This research programme has considerably influenced post-adjustment development economics.

Section II

The Return to the Founding Fathers

The work that aimed to return to the thinking of development pioneers began by noting the decline of their approach from the middle of the 1970s, in favour of orthodox analyses (Krugman 1993). According to these analysts, this decline can be explained by the failures of development and by the low standard of formalisation in the founding models of development theory (Krugman 1995).

Recent economic research findings, however, are tending to confirm the intuitions and the recommendations of several pioneering studies on a number of issues. Regarding international trade, the research of the early development theorists demonstrated that international openness and integration into the world economy were unfavourable to underdeveloped countries. For instance, G. Myrdal showed that the spread of technical progress and growth from developed countries to underdeveloped countries, which could be inferred from the Hecksher-Ohlin model, was cancelled out by holdback effects (Myrdal 1957).During the same decade, ECLA studies, particularly by Prebisch and Singer, on the deterioration of terms of trade in underdeveloped countries, because of their participation in international trade, exercised considerable influence on development theorists, and justified the elaboration of import-substitution strategies aimed at the domestic market.

These ideas were strongly criticised with the return in force of neo-liberal thinking and the comparative-advantage approach in the 1970s. More particularly, research on "effective protection rates" and "domestic resource cost" sought to demonstrate that protection of industrial sectors,

27

especially heavy industry, penalised them, by keeping them out of global competition, which could have motivated them to increase their competitiveness. Furthermore, according to the critics of introverted growth models, protectionism also penalised exports, agriculture and light industry (Balassa 1971; Little et al. 1970).

Neo-liberal criticism was strengthened in the 1970s with the difficulties and limitations that affected import-substitution strategies. A number of studies increasingly stressed the positive correlation between exports and economic growth (Michaely 1977, Balassa 1978). The introverted approaches of the pioneers of development theory were particularly challenged in the 1970s in studies by Krueger (1978) and Bhagwati (1978). Their research examined the effects and consequences of exchange rate liberalisation policies and the reduction of customs duties in 10 countries between 1952 and 1972. It also demonstrated that devaluation does not have an inflationary effect, and that liberalisation is necessary to encourage exports. These studies, and the debt crisis, had a major impact on development strategies in the developing world from the early 1980s onward. The recommendations of the early pioneers were set aside in favour of more liberal policies that encouraged international integration according to the comparative advantages of underdeveloped countries.

Recent research on international trade, however, diverges from the presentations of neo-liberal theories. The point of departure of the new theories on international trade is a criticism of comparative advantage theory and its inability to make sense of international relations. More specifically, the traditional theory of international trade does not provide a satisfactory explanation for the fact that the bulk of trade takes place between developed countries with comparable levels of technology and factor endowments, and involves similar products (Hellier 1993).

28

This criticism of the traditional comparative advantage theory has given rise to what is commonly referred to as the "new theory of international trade" (Greenaway 1987; Helpman and Razin 1991; Krugman 1990). Although the early work of this new trend dates back to the end of the 1970s, these developments only became the new dominant paradigm in the debate on international trade in the mid-1980s. In this body of work, P. Krugman looks into the effects of non-constant returns on international specialisation and uneven development between countries (Krugman 1981). P. Krugman develops a model based on two countries and two sectors (agriculture and industry), and considers economies of scale, external to the firm, in the industrial sector. The two countries begin to trade with each other, according to the principles of comparative advantage. However, economies of scale give the country with the most capital stock a cost advantage, which promotes the accumulation of capital and strengthens its initial advantage. According to this model, economies of scale are responsible for cumulative growth and competitiveness, which leads to a monopoly in industrial goods. In the longer term, the country with more capital stock specialises in industrial production, while the other is locked into an agricultural-exporting economy.

Other authors have examined trade policies on international markets with imperfect competition (Brander 1981; Brander and Krugman 1983; Brander and Spencer 1985). They recommend that economies adopt strategic trade policies aimed at increasing foreign markets for national firms. Authors such as J. A. Brander and B. Spencer favour strong government intervention in favour of national enterprises, by means of taxes and export subsidies, and by defining a fiscal policy that penalises foreign exporters. The new theories of international trade criticise traditional theories and demonstrate that free trade is not an optimum solution for economies.

These conclusions are, however, qualified by P. Krugman, who considers that it is difficult to define an alternative policy to free trade, and that support for free trade should continue, even though it is a second-rate solution (Krugman 1993). Thus, while free trade may be no better than protectionist strategy, it is easier to implement and leads therefore to fewer distortions. So, while he departs from the neo-liberals in his analysis, P. Krugman and the other adherents of the new international trade theories join comparative advantage theorists in recommending the implementation of free trade policies in international trade.

In addition to work on international trade, the return to the work of the founding fathers also concerns the issue of economies of scale. We should point out that early work on development economics stressed the importance and role of economies of scale in the dynamics of economic development. With his "Big Push" theory, P. Rosenstein-Rodan was one of the first authors to consider that economies of scale on the microeconomic level and the supply of labour in underdeveloped countries could lead to strong growth dynamics (Rodan 1943, 1961). Economies of scale are also stressed in the work of A. Hirschman (Hirschman 1964). In his reflection on unbalanced growth, he points out that the idea of economies of scale is central to inter-industrial liaisons. During the same period, the issue of economies of scale was also studied, to varying extents, by development theorists such as Nurkse, Scitovsky, Lewis and Myrdal, who were interested in understanding how to transform economies of scale at the microeconomic level in underdeveloped economies into increasing returns at the level of the national economy (Krugman 1993).

From the middle of the 1960s, however, the issue of economies of scale was set aside, with the return in force of neoclassical theory and the hypothesis of increasing returns in traditional growth theories. The neoclassical model of growth was based on Solow's work, which sought to construct a model of stable growth based on Walrassian hypotheses (Solow 1956). According to that model and its extensions, growth can only proceed from population growth and from increased labour productivity, stemming from exogenous technical progress. In these models, investment does not influence growth since, as stipulated by neoclassical theory, physical capital has diminishing incremental returns and constant returns to scale; in this framework, the profitability of investments decreases along with capital stock. From this point of view, the rate of accumulation cannot overtake the growth of the workforce and its level of efficiency.

These models of growth faced considerable criticism from the middle of the 1980s, because of their inability to explain the evolution of growth dynamics in recent years. In the first place, these theories cannot explain the catch-up phenomena at work in the world economy, and more particularly the fact that even if a certain number of developed and developing countries have not succeeded in organising coherent production systems, they have still experienced strong growth in productivity, which has enabled them to approach American productivity levels (Henin and Ralle 1994). Furthermore, the traditional framework is unable to explain the slowing down of productivity in the present crisis, despite the increased rate of technical progress. Since the beginning of the 1970s, there has been a sharp rise in research and development expenditure in developed countries, along with the progressive establishment of a new technological paradigm, following the decline of the Ford technical model. However, despite these changes, productivity has not resumed the strong growth it enjoyed in the 1950s and 1960s.

For these reasons, there was a revival of growth theories in the mid-1980s, concentrating notably on increasing returns, which marked a return to the work of the founders of development economics, such as P. Rosenstein-Rodan and A. Hirschman. Neoclassical theory cannot by definition include increasing returns in its theoretical schema. Factor increases cause higher than proportionate increases in the volume of production, and producers have no reason to restrict production, since they are sure to be able to sell their products. Based on this, production will tend towards infinity, and in situations of pure and perfect competition, it becomes difficult to resolve the producers' optimisation problem.

Since it is difficult to sustain this hypothesis, Romer (1986) modified it by introducing increasing returns, using Marshall's logic. Romer argued that the internal conditions of production within enterprises are conditions of non-increasing returns. He envisaged increasing returns from the size of the market or the national economy, which had a positive external effect on capital and encouraged firms to invest. This accumulation of capital led to an increase in the firm's productive capacity; this is the effect on capital. In addition, it had beneficial effects on the acquisition of skills and on increasing know-how within the firm (something that Romer refers to as "learning spillover"), which is transmitted to the rest of the economy through inter-business links. Thehypothesis of increasing returns is introduced into the analysis in this way, while preserving the fundamental principle of pure and perfect competition.

In this model, the growth path closely depends on the elasticity of production and total knowledge. If elasticity is less than 1, the model retains the basic properties of Solow's model and growth tends towards zero. However, when elasticity is equal to 1, Romer demonstrates the possibility of a growth path at constant rates, relatively close to the growth path resulting from exogenous technical progress. Finally, if elasticity is greater than 1, growth will occur at increasing rates.

Romer's model also demonstrates that the situation of competitive equilibrium is sub-optimal. Firms do not include the implications of global economic interdependence in their plans and thus do not obtain all the benefits they could from the positive external effect. When they develop their production plans in the context of decentralised economies, firms only consider the marginal productivity of knowledge, equal to f'_k in the production function f(k,K), which is clearly inferior to productivity in social optimum calculations ($f'_k + Nf'_k$) (Amable and Guellec 1992). Investment stemming from market equilibrium would be lower than investment corresponding to the social optimum. Hence the importance of government intervention to make private interests compatible with collective interests.

A return to the work of the founders of development economics is also seen in the emphasis which endogenous growth theories place on the accumulation of human capital and the importance of access to and mastery of new technology. P. Romer stresses the role of technological innovations and R. Lucas focuses on the accumulation of human capital in explaining the dynamics of economic growth. In Romer's model, growth from additional investments is not endogenous to factors of production and constitutes an additional factor that enables economies of scale to contribute to growth. R. Lucas tries to overcome this limitation by analysing human capital as an aspect of labour, which allows a clear improvement of the productive capacities of the labour force (Lucas 1988). According to Lucas, the accumulation of human capital may come from learning phenomena, such as "learning by doing", or as a result of training programmes to which workers devote part of their working time, in order to improve their performance, and thus increase their earnings.

Lucas demonstrates that the combination of an accumulation of knowledge with constant marginal efficiency and the external effect of human capital allows economies to experience sustained growth. However, Lucas observes that the growth rate of human capital in an optimum situation is higher than in an equilibrium situation. He thus observes the same gap between the equilibrium and the optimum, highlighted by Romer's model, which stems from the inability of private agents to incorporate the surplus of social efficiency from the accumulation of human capital into their plans. From this angle, the decisions of economic operators about the accumulation of human capital are determined by private considerations of increased satisfaction, and do not take into consideration the collective consequences of the accumulation of human capital. This gap between optimum and equilibrium justifies government intervention in the form of subsidies for educational systems and training and research organisations.

Lucas' model also offers some explanations for uneven development among nations. His model shows that an initial discrepancy in the endowment of different nations with physical and human capital tends to continue and even widen. These findings focus our attention on the importance of the investments underdeveloped countries should make, to increase physical and human capital and reduce the discrepancies in development, which divide them from developed countries.

Endogenous growth theories that attempt to revive thinking on development by returning to the works of the founding fathers have had a considerable influence on development studies. R. J. Barro sought

34

to determine the factors that influenced growth dynamics in 116 . economies between 1965 and 1985 (Barro and Lee 1994). This study demonstrated once again the importance of the factors that have been highlighted by different theories of endogenous growth, such as GDP/ per head, education, health, the share of investments in income, the scope of the government and political stability. Other authors have examined growth factors in Africa over the 1960-1987 period (Savvides 1995). R. Lucas looked into factors that restrict the flow of investments from developed countries to underdeveloped countries (Lucas 1990). He particularly noted differences in endowment in human capital, market imperfections and political stability.

Endogenous growth theories have thus inspired one school of post-adjustment development economics to seek to renew development theories by returning to the work of the founding fathers. This has enabled these authors to break away from the Walrassian model. Indeed, these new presentations challenge the basic model by recognising the sub-optimal nature of equilibrium and by stressing the importance of government intervention to correct imperfections. However, while they may in theory recognise the importance of the role of government in optimising growth, they refuse to include it in their recommendations (Romer 1993). In fact, all these authors criticise all forms of interventionism in the regulation of underdeveloped economies, because of the difficulty of drawing up and implementing such policies. Laissez-faire remains the best solution for these authors, even though it is only a second best. Thus, despite a profound criticism of the Walrassian theoretical framework, this approach to post-adjustment development economics remains a prisoner of neo-liberal theories in terms of recommendations and development strategy.

The ambiguity in these analyses is also apparent when applied to the Newly Industrialised Countries (NICs) of Southeast Asia. After studying these economies, P. Krugman came to the conclusion that we were looking at a myth based on low labour costs, and that these economies would not stand up to international competition and would collapse fairly quickly (Krugman 1994). This analysis seems to be contradicted by the facts and by recent interpretations of the experiences of Southeast Asian countries, which, on the contrary, despite the recent crisis, stress the profound changes in the productive structures of these countries. These changes are a result of adaptation and mastery of new technologies. Thus, instead of seizing on these economies to demonstrate the accuracy of their views and to justify their theoretical analyses on international trade, the advocates of the new theories of international trade seek to minimise the experiences of the NICs.

The adherents of these new theories deliberately maintain this ambiguity between analyses and recommendations. Although they develop more relevant analyses of international trade and economic growth, these economists do not break their ties with the Walrassian framework and continue to identify themselves with the dominant party in the field of economic theory. These studies thus refuse to analyse and understand the changes and transitions in progress in the developing world and treat the Southeast Asian NICs as exporters of cheaplabour-intensive products, like the economies of Tunisia, Morocco or Mauritius. This refusal to understand the uniqueness of these countries' experience cannot even be justified by a desire to preserve links with the neoclassical school, since most neo-liberal theories today accept the role played by various institutions and non-market interventions in the "success" of the NICs.

Section III

The New Institutional Economics

Development economics, like the new microeconomics, has seen challenges to the basic hypotheses of the Walrassian model. The need for increased relevance has led to abandonment of the strict model's hypotheses of perfect competition and information, and development studies have begun to examine the imperfections of the market. These imperfections suggest the need for further research on institutions and mechanisms that correct the market's regulating action in decentralised economies. These concerns were behind the renewal of work on institutions with the New Institutional Economics (NIE) or new institutionalism. This line of research also developed in development economics and has progressively come to dominate recent work on underdeveloped economies.

The development of this line of thought has been influenced by the neo-Keynesians and the synthesis which they attempted to make between macroeconomic concerns and the microeconomic bases for the actions of economic operators[2]. The development of the neo- Keynesian movement in the 1980s was based on opposition to the theory of rational expectations about the ability of decentralised economies to achieve equilibrium. According to expectation theory, price adjustment ensures market equilibrium, whereas according to the neo- Keynesians, prices are "sticky", and adjustment of prices to quantities is relatively slow. The neo- Keynesiansargue that it is this price "stickiness"that is responsible for rigidities in the market. However, although initial

---

[2]   In this respect, it should be noted that several advocates of the new institutional economics, such as J. E. Stiglitz, come from the neo-Keynesian movement.

synthesis economists only point out the existence of rigidities, the neo-Keynesians attempt to give them a microeconomic explanation. The neo- Keynesians uphold the paradoxical hypothesis that rigidities are the result of rational behaviour by economic agents in imperfect market conditions.

The neo-Keynesian revival is essentially opposed to the theory of rational expectations with respect to two issues. The first point is epistemological in nature and involves the eternal debate between relevance and rigour, and the coherence of theories (Blinder 1979). While the neo- Keynesian theory recognises the rigour of rational expectations, it nevertheless stresses their unrealistic nature. Certain authors have, therefore, opted for a research problematic aimed at increasing the relevance of the neo- Keynesian theory, through a more in-depth study of rigidities and their macroeconomic consequences. There has been some work to show that, in menu cost issues, rigidities may result from rational behaviour by firms, given the cost of price adjustment. Some research has shown that price rigidity is more generally the norm in capitalist economies than flexibility (Carlton 1986).

The second issue addressed by the neo- Keynesian economics involves the postulate of the rationality of operators in rational expectations. The neo- Keynesians' criticism of rationality does not apply to the basic core of neo-classical theory, especially equilibrium and the market. The criticism addresses the "radical" and exclusive nature of the postulate in rational expectations. Through their study of the labour market, the neo-Keynesians point to the considerable complexity of relationships between economic operators , which should lead economists to qualify the postulate of rationality. A number of studies on efficiency wages consider that a real wage higher than the equilibrium wage may have positive repercussions on productivity (Katz 1986; Krueger and Summers 1988). Other work on implicit contracts has demonstrated the existence of implicit relationships and strict standards, established among workers or between workers and management, alongside the relationships codified in collective bargaining (Taylor 1980). Beyond these divergences from rational expectation theory, the goal of the neo-Keynesians is not so much a revival of the *General Theory,* as it is an attempt to reconcile the Keynesian method with the neoclassical model. The methodological choice of individualism and the consideration of contractual procedures in the regulation of societies are at the core of the synthesis between Keynesian and neoclassical methods.

This theoretical evolution has had major consequences on development practices and strategies. Authors increasingly challenge the liberal recommendations of the Washington consensus. J. E. Stiglitz, the new chief economist of the World Bank, notes that development experiences in Southeast Asia have demonstrated the importance of government intervention in regulating a market economy (Stiglitz 1997). This new development practice views the market as the most important institution for regulating the projects of different operators in a decentralised economy. According to that conception, however, market imperfections require corrective interventions by the government (Datta-Chadhuri 1990). In this respect, J. E. Stiglitz believes the government should intervene in six areas in modern economies (Stiglitz 1997). The first area of government intervention is the promotion of education. According to J. E. Stiglitz, universal education creates the conditions for a more just and egalitarian society. The government should also play a major role in developing new technologies. Stiglitz points out that in the United States, new technologies, including the electronic communications networks, have been developed by the government.

The third area of government intervention involves the financial sector. Stiglitz notes that, in Asian countries, the government ensured the stability of the financial system and allowed the creation of the necessary institutions to finance growth dynamics. The government should also intervene in the development of basic infrastructures, such as roads and communications systems. Government intervention is also important in preventing environmental degradation. Finally, according to J. E. Stiglitz, the government has a role to play in the satisfaction of the population's basic needs, particularly healthcare. .

Alongside these changes and evolutions in development practices and strategies, however, and their divergence from the Washington consensus on adjustment, theoretical practices have developed which, under the influence of the new microeconomics and NIE, emphasise market imperfections and take an interest in the institutions involved in the regulation of decentralised economies.

A number of theoretical trends and practices, which identify themselves with institutionalism, have emerged in the field of development economics. The point of departure for all these new institutional approaches is the inability of pure Walrassian equilibrium to deal with the uniqueness of accumulation and behaviour of economic operators in underdeveloped countries. According to these authors, markets are less harmonious in developing countries, the division of the labour market is very deep, and the situation of extreme poverty leads operators to behave in ways that do not conform to the postulates of the basic Walrassian model. J.C. Berthélemy, J. G. Devezeaux de Lavergne and F. Gagey note that, "under the influence of factors that are unusual in rich countries, economic rationality can lead to reactions that appear paradoxical to the pricing system" (Berthélemy 1991).

J. E. Stiglitz lists a series of stylised facts in Third World countries that cannot be analysed by standard theory, including (Stiglitz 1988):

- tremendous urban unemployment, which makes it appear that wages are higher than market equilibrium wages,

- considerable wage differences for relatively similar levels of qualification,

- considerable migration from rural areas to urban areas despite urban unemployment,

- modes of distribution based on principles of sharing and community participation, especially in the rural environment, rather than on productivity.

Questioning the ability of the pure model to make sense of concrete realities in underdeveloped countries has not led to a break between the new institutionalism and the basic model. On the contrary, NIE in the field of development is an extension of neoclassical theory, to the extent that it seeks to explain institutions by the microeconomic behaviour of operators (Yong 1994). From this standpoint, institutions allow operators to maximise their behaviour in a context of imperfect information and competition. NIE can thus be distinguished from J. R. Commons' conception, which seeks the foundations of collective behaviour through an analysis of institutions. In NIE, institutions are restricted to the study of forms of co-ordination among operators as a result of market imperfections.

The diversity of the new institutional approaches can be observed through an analysis of the different definitions of institutions proposed by different authors. D. North establishes a distinction between institution and organisation. According to this analysis, institutions represent all the formal rules (laws, etc.) and informal constraints conceived by people, which form the structure of incentives in an economy (North 1994). Organisations, on the other hand, are conceived by D. North as individuals or groups of individuals. Interactions between institutions and organisations are the foundation for social change. This distinction between organisation and institution is not taken up by authors such as M. Nabli and J. B. Nugent, who define an institution as a set of rules and constraints that govern behaviour and relationships between individuals or groups (Nabli and Nugent 1989). From this viewpoint, organisations such as labour unions, various markets, implicit or explicit contracts and codes of cultural behaviour are seen as institutions, since they produce standards of behaviour for individuals or groups of individuals. According to J. E. Stiglitz, institutions include rules and operational standards, as well as organisations such as the family or the market (Stiglitz 1988)...

The diversity of NIE resides essentially in the conceptions and aspects, which different authors stress in their analysis of institutions.

Institutionalism and transaction costs

Certain authors focus on R. H. Coase and O. Williamson's transaction cost approach, which considers that, in the context of an imperfect market, businesses seek to internalise a great many activities in order to save on costs generated by recourse to the outside (Basu 1984). This theory has not been much developed, because of criticisms mainly of its descriptive character and its lack of an operational definition of the notion of transaction costs.

Institutionalism and social change

This theory is an extension of D. North's work on economic history. North places institutions at the centre of the evolution of different economies and views them as the foundation for the decadence or the prosperity of nations (North 1988). According to this conception, development is defined as growth dynamics with effective institutional change.

According to North, relative price changes are the foundation for institutional change, since they lead economic actors to define new contractual and institutional arrangements. North's theory of institutions includes three levels of analysis:

- a theory of the rights of property and organisation, which, according to North, helps the problems of incentives and information in a market economy,

- a theory of government, which, according to North, plays a central role since it defines and implements property rights,

- a theory of ideology that justifies and explains actors' behaviour and especially induces them to control their individualistic actions and makes them more sensitive to equilibrium and social stability.

North's ideas on institutions have led to the development of a considerable body of work in development economics. W. Ruttan and Y. Hayami, for instance, developed the theory of institutional innovation induced by interactions between supply and demand (Ruttan and Hayami 1984). D. Feeny showed that the rising price of land in Thailand from 1850 onwards and its opening up to international trade led to stronger land property rights and the abandonment of slavery (Feeny 1979). Other authors, such as M. Bently and T. Oberhofer, observed similar developments in West Africa, with increased demand for institutional change following economic development and an increase in productivity under the impact of technical change (Bently and Oberhofer 1981).

Institutionalism and imperfect information

This is the largest school of institutionalist thought, which wields considerable influence in the field of development theory. This approach seeks to understand the formation of institutions through the rational behaviour of economic operators The imperfect nature of economic information explains imperfections in market operations, which different actors seek to minimise, by implementing a multitude of contracts and microeconomic organisations (Bardhan 1993).

The most representative work of this school is thatof J. E. Stiglitz. His theory of imperfect information is based on five central hypotheses (Stiglitz 1988, 1986, and 1985):

- economic operators are rational,

- information has a cost, and therefore, individuals do not have perfect information at their disposal,

- institutions are endogenous and represent the response of operators s to problems of access to information,

- the economy is not efficient in Pareto's sense of the word, which means operators adapt and sometimes act in ways that contradict classic rationality,

- in this situation of imperfect information, the government must play a major role to promote the co-ordination of maximising behaviour by operators and so make up for market imperfections.

In this theory, an examination of situations of imperfect information is the point of departure for studying development problems and analysing the behaviour of economic operators in underdeveloped economies. This approach has shown a particular interest in the behaviour of peasants in Third World countries, which classical analyses viewed as irrational. Contrary to the standard line of thought, institutional economists have shown that the contractual forms developed by peasants at the grassroots level constitute rational responses to market imperfections, and especially to the uncertainty surrounding the rural environment in underdeveloped countries, because of technological backwardness and the lack of any form of support from the public authorities (Bardhan 1989; Binswanger and Rosenzweig 1984; Eswaran and Kotwal 1985; Stiglitz 1988).

This school has studied other themes, such as the experiences of Southeast Asian countries (Chang 1993; Haggard 1990). According to T. Cheng, S. Haggard and D. Kang, the transition towards a system of promotion of exports in Asian countries required the formation of a series of institutions, which strengthened the government and its ability to formulate and implement its strategies (Cheng et al. 1996). According to these authors, despite differences in their development strategies, Asian countries organised four types of institutions, which contributed considerably to their growth dynamics:

- the first institution involves the constitutional system, which defined the connections and relationships between the different political actors. In most countries, this was an authoritarian system in which powers were concentrated,
- the establishment of an organised and highly qualified government bureaucracy,
- the role played by different negotiating and arbitration organisations involving governments and the business community. These

institutions helped solve problems of information and facilitated the dialogue necessary to work out development strategies and policies,

- strong state institutions, which played a dynamic role in these countries' rapid industrialisation , especially industrial development boards and sectorial institutions (heavy industry boards, export councils and other export organisations...).

J. Stiglitz also looked into the growth dynamics of Asian countries (Stiglitz 1996). In his analysis, he stressed the need for government intervention in incomplete and imperfect markets. According to Stiglitz, inadequate markets are important in underdeveloped countries, and require government intervention as the experience of Asian countries has shown, to correct their imperfections and to ensure a greater co-ordination of the strategic actions of different operators.

Government action has been particularly decisive in the financial sector in Asian countries, because imperfection is more serious in that market and can threaten development efforts. J. Stiglitz lists a series of imperfections in the financial market that call for regulating intervention by the government (Stiglitz 1994). Public authorities in Asian countries contributed to the creation of a financial system and various financing institutions. They also closely regulated the operations of financial markets by directing funds to certain industrial activities and not to others (Stiglitz 1996).

To sum up, this branch of NIE has played an important role in challenging the pure Walrassian model, by demonstrating its inability to analyse and understand the unique behaviours of economic operators in situations of imperfect competition and information. These studies contributed to the criticism of the consensus that had dominated development economics since the beginning of the 1980s. While this branch of NIE criticises traditional microeconomics, it does not, however, cut all ties with liberalism, as its theoretical methods are an extension of the new Walrassian microeconomics and aim to enrich the basic model by giving it the means to understand and analyse market imperfections linked to imperfect information. Institutions are thus analysed as a product of maximising and rational behaviour by those operating in imperfect markets. This is a reductionist view, which limits institutions to arrangements and rules, which operators establish in situations of imperfect information. The approach is marked by methodological individualism, and its analytical scope excludes the collective behaviour, which the founding fathers of the institutional school of thought favoured in the works of R. Commons. P. Bardhan points out that these analyses ignore the power relationships and struggles within institutions, which lead to an unequal sharing of property rights (Bardhan 1989).

In the field of development, NIE cannot easily explain and analyse the genesis of institutions (creation and renewal). Indeed, most contributions are limited to a synchronic vision of institutions, trying to describe them and understand the role they play in the dynamics of accumulation and economic growth. The dynamics of the creation and evolution of institutions are rarely analysed. For example, with respect to transition dynamics in Third-World countries, NIE holds that the efficiency of the institutions set up in Asian countries is responsible for these countries' dynamic and competitive integration into the world economy. This approach does not explain why these economies were able to develop efficient institutions and why other Third-World countries have not been able to follow the same pattern. In other words, we need to understand the underlying causes of the inefficiency of institutions in most Third-World countries except in Southeast Asia. NIE merely describes

47

institutions which are supposed to function efficiently in certain countries, without proposing means and mechanisms to improve the performance of institutions in other countries, so as to promote a revival of growth dynamics and of dynamic integration into the international economy.

In conclusion, while the new institutional economics allows us to enrich the pure equilibrium model in development studies by increasing its relevance, it does not equip us to analyse the dynamics in progress in the Third World, and particularly the different transitions occurring since the mid-eighties. Nor does this school of thought live up to expectations in terms of development strategies, in the context of the crisis of the nation-state and the increased opening of national economies to the international economy.

Relativisation of rationality

Several works , especially in French, have examined the relativisation of the rationality of economic actors subject to social and economic determinism. This work challenges the ability of traditional microeconomics to grasp these specific modes of behaviour, and attempts to explain the gap between the rationality of these actors and Walrassian rationality. This work has dealt with African economies and has attempted to deal with theories on the irrationality of African economic actors. "Economic irrationality", according to Ph. Hugon, "is linked to the degree of priority given the symbolic dimension of actions. The value of persons and interpersonal relationships is greater than the value of things" (Hugon 1995).

These studies have stressed African economic operators' submission to two systems of determination: the community system, which binds them to their home community through a series of obligations, and the individual system, in which economic agents attempt to fulfil their subjective needs. It is against this background that Ph. Hugon writes that, "What is a virtue according to community logic (polygamy, solidarity, respect for ancestors), becomes a vice, according to the logic of efficiency:- nepotism, patronage, tribalism" (Hugon 1995).

This overlapping of two types of reasoning has major consequences on development studies, particularly about the viability of statistical systems, which are essentially based on individual systems of determination, and do not account for the weight of community logic in actors' behaviour. Indeed, "The statistical methods used," says F.-R. Mahieu, "are based on an individual representation of social determinations. Individualism in this case is only one method for representing the impact of social factors on individual behaviour." (Mahieu 1995).

This approach makes the community an important social institution, which plays an important role in mitigating the impact of uncertainty and instability in Africa. From a theoretical point of view, this approach is close to the French conventionalist approach, which seeks to move beyond standard theory and extended standard theory and to construct a new conception of the socialisation of actors, by taking institutions and conventions into consideration (Hammouda 1997). In the study of conventions in underdeveloped economies, O. Favereau distinguishes three levels of analysis (Favereau 1995):

1.   the agents' individual rationality

In this context, O. Favereau considers that decision-making criteria differ and change from one polity to another. Furthermore, each polity develops its own mechanisms and procedures for the social management of uncertainty. "We will consider," writes O. Favereau, "rules of decision-making to be a priori no more and no less rational in African economies than in European economies, on condition that we admit that decisions are rational within the framework of socially constructed formulations of decision-making problems. The uniqueness of African economies (sub-Saharan Africa) should be sought in the type of socialisation of uncertainty, and more specifically, in the possible preponderance of the Domestic Polity e over the other Polities , in the social inscription of individual rationalities" (Favereau 1995:186). In African societies, O. Favereau concurs with R. Mahieu's hypothesis of the decisive role played by community standards on the behaviour of individual actors.

2. the businesses

O. Favereau begins by pointing out the principal characteristics of African businesses, including poor management and the prevalence of corruption. These characteristics are a result of the preponderance of social institutions (such as community rule) in motivating the individual behaviour of economic operators. In this context, African businesses are a centre of production, which aims to redistribute the wealth they create rather than to accumulate it. Furthermore, the domination of the Commercial Polity by the Domestic Polity can be observed in African businesses, which attempt to reproduce social relationships external to them, thus further weakening them.

3. the equilibrium of rules

In order to analyse co-ordination as a whole, O. Favereau uses the conventionalists' idea of a balance of rules, which examines economic operators' rules of adaptation and adjustment. This idea leads him to suggest that the model of operation of African businesses cannot lead to strong growth. In fact, according to Favereau, "African societies' microeconomic modes of adaptation to uncertainty tend to increase macroeconomic uncertainty, by making the economy more vulnerable to conjunctural crises, crises of supply and crises of demand" (Favereau 1995:195). In O. Favereau's view, SAPs, which attempt to reduce deficits, should be reinforced, and local agents should be taught standards of efficiency by organisational reforms, so as to overcome the institutional obstacles, which characterise these societies.

In their criticism of standard microeconomic studies, conventionalist analyses do not stray from their normative methodology. Indeed, their work switches between scientific analysis and normative discourse on development. These analyses advance the hypothesis of the superiority of capitalist management standards over all other forms or standards of management. The objective of the analysis is no longer to understand the underlying reasons for economic crises in Africa, but to demonstrate that the crisis is the result of lack of conformity of operators' behaviour with what is supposed to be the rational standard of behaviour. Seen in this light, the goal of development strategy is to bring the behaviour of operators closer to the capitalist standard, which is seen as an ideal model of efficiency, and to break away from the grassroots solidarity that African societies have been able to maintain, despite the violent penetration of commercial relationships during the colonial period. From this point of view, the violence of adjustment, which sought to reduce social regulation by the state, does not go far enough and should be reinforced by other forms of action against grassroots solidarity, which is viewed as a serious obstacle to development.

The study of the community as an institution that plays an important role in the socialisation of African economic operators is central to F.

51

R. Mahieu's research. He considers that, "economic theory is confronted with particularities in African economic behaviour at two levels: the microeconomic level of the relationship with the community and the macroeconomic level of the relationship between the state and these same communities" (Mahieu 1990). At the microeconomic level, African economic operators are subject to community constraints, which, according to these analyses, are superimposed on the maximising individualistic logic of the pure equilibrium model. "Survival thus depends," according to F. R. Mahieu," not only on individual rights (and the corresponding trade list), but above all on community rights, which are conditioned by obligations towards the self-same community" (Mahieu 1990:12).

In order to analyse the community, F. R. Mahieu introduces the ideas of rights and obligations. From this point of view, the community is made up of a dense network of rights and obligations between individuals. The foundations of the community are not restricted to economic aspects, but also include political, religious and other motivations, which are more closely linked to the imaginary and symbolic world . In this world, each individual has an individual list of rights and obligations towards his or her community. This list gives rise to exchanges and transfers between individuals. From this point of view, African societies appear as societies of a community imposed on its members and of community transfers. These exchanges may lead to disequilibrium, since certain individuals may receive more than they give. "This situation," explains F. R. Mahieu, "of credit or debit with respect to the community depends largely on the individual's position in the history of the community" (Mahieu 1990:122).

This system of rights and obligations draws its strength from the system of sanctions that communities set in place to impose strict respect for community standards on every individual. Furthermore, the community represents for each individual a refuge and a guarantee in periods of uncertainty. According to the author, this conception constitutes a radical criticism of the analyses of the World Bank, which, "by refusing to step outside the framework of the market, shut themselves up in the economic theory of rational households and totally bypass the reality of the community " (Mahieu 1990:23).

Community relationships do not, however, stop at the microeconomic level, they also involve a macroeconomic dimension in the relations between the state and the various communities that form the nation-state. There too, according to F. R. Mahieu, community constraints and community transfers are central to relations between the state and citizens. According to this, the state's various social expenditures should be analysed through the prism of community constraints and transfers that have to be made to different communities.

Despite its intention of breaking away from the neoclassical framework and from the standard analyses of the World Bank, this approach is still marked by an a-historical and static analysis. In its essentialist analytical grid, community constraints appear as a characteristic outside time, and are therefore unaffected by historical evolution. A number of studies have pointed out the destructuring of community relationships in African countries since colonial times. To introduce export crops, colonial authorities reformed local fiscal systems, particularly by imposing taxes in cash. These economic changes were at the root of the development of commercial relationships, which began to erode community relationships (Hammouda 1993). This process continued in the post-colonial period, with attempts to reform the modern state and with the emergence of an urban middle class, which began to free itself from its community ties, and formed the core for the emergence of the autonomous individual. Community relations have not, of course, completely disappeared, but in the face of these changes, their impact has become increasingly formal.

The idea of community constraints is not a new one in the study of African communities. As far back as 1957, in his analysis of the historical evolution of societies, S. Amin was the first to introduce the hypothesis of a succession of three modes of production, the community family, the tributary family and the capitalist mode, as an alternative to the hypotheses of the Asian mode of production or the succession of five modes of production (Amin 1979, 1996). According to Amin, the succession of these three forms of social organisation occurred through two basic events. The first was responsible for the transition from the community mode to the tributary mode. In community society, land ownership was established on a community basis and kinship ideology dominated society and played an important role in maintaining it. In tributary societies, social power was crystallised within state cores, which dominated economic activities and land ownership. Under community and tributary systems, economic activities are marked by the value of tradition and attach little importance to commercial exchanges. Tributary authorities legitimise their social control in the metaphysical and religious ideological world. The second major change involved the transition from tributary societies to capitalism, with the development of commercial relations and the private appropriation of the means of production and an economic ideology.

The argument developed by S. Amin was a simple research hypothesis, which we should continue to question, particularly with regards to "failed" transitions towards capitalism in certain underdeveloped societies, such as the Arab world or Africa. But it has an advantage over the neo- communitarian theories in that it provides a dynamic and historical grid of explanation, which does not stop at a mere empirical observation of the importance of the community in Africa, but attempts to understand and analyse it. In parallel with the difficulties acknowledged by F. R. Mahieu in setting up a community formula to replace the Walrassian formula (Mahieu 1990), the community as a microeconomic constraint has stood the test of time, and despite the mutations and evolutions of African societies and their legitimising world, continues to explain the behaviour of individuals and economic actors.

The analyses of the neo- communitarian macroeconomic school of thought also pose certain difficulties and evoke criticism.It should be pointed out in the first place that this conception of macroeconomic relations is limited to mutual transfers between the state and the different communities. Everything seems to take place in the best of all worlds, to the extent that what the state levies from the different communities is returned through agricultural development programmes or other types of state expenditures, particularly social spending. This interpretation, which does not include power struggles between the state and the different communities, is contradicted by present-day facts. Firstly, democratic openness and the questioning of authoritarian power have demonstrated that African states, after a brief modernist period, have turned inwards to their leaders' ethnic or regional communities, to the exclusion of the other communities. Thus, while certain communities have benefited from certain transfers, others have been totally excluded from the distribution of the fruits of the economic growth of the 1960s and 1970s. This political and economic exclusion partly explains the identity-based nature of the movement protesting against the political monopoly of the African state in the 1980s.

Neo- communitarian theorists seem also to minimise the impact of state levies on peasants, especially since they consider that state transfers feed into community solidarity networks. This analysis is contradicted by precise studies and field surveys in different African economies (Cochet 1996). This work shows that, on the contrary, levies on peasants have played an important role in setting up state structures and have obstructed accumulation on farms, thus engendering low agricultural productivity. The limitation of the modernisation of agricultural productive structures and low levels of agricultural surplus meant that, from the mid-1970s, African states went into debt, in order to continue to fund growth dynamics. State investment in agriculture was rarely directed at improving agricultural productivity, however, especially that of subsistence crops. On the contrary, agricultural development efforts in the 1970s were aimed at export crops, which produced income to feed government budgets. Relations between the state and the communities have thus nothing in common with the smooth, stable image conveyed by the neo- communitarian theorists. On the contrary, the study of state/community relations places us at the heart of mechanisms of control and social domination exercised by the state over African peasants..

The neo-communitarian theorists explain low agricultural productivity by community constraints. According to these theorists, African peasants attribute greater importance to community time and social activities than to productive activities, which leads to a negative impact on agricultural productivity. F. R. Mahieu notes that "several perverse effects intervene in the allocation of time for productivity, because of the priority given to community time and the particular value of formal work in relation to the community. Any attack on the distribution structure has chain effects on the substitution of informal activities for formal activities and on reduced productivity" (Mahieu 1990:86).

56

In this analysis, reduced agricultural productivity and the stagnation of agricultural development are essentially due to the inadequate means of production available on African farms. Equipment is not very diversified, limited as it is to hoes, machetes and a few baskets. The availability of these tools is problematical, since industrial development as envisaged in most African countries after independence, has paid little heed to co-ordination with agriculture. Furthermore, since transportation equipment is not well developed, in most cases, peasants carry their produce, which is not without consequences on the availability of labour input on farms. In addition, fertilisers and pesticides are rarely used, as they are seldom available and are relatively expensive. Finally, there is little variety in the biological material available to peasants (Hammouda 1995).

These factors, taken together, are responsible for the low productivity of labour and especially the difficulties reported in many African countries during work peaks, contrary to the affirmations of communitarian theorists regarding the time peasants spend on community obligations. The main consequence of peasants' low labour capacity, because of inadequate equipment, has been a restriction of the surface area farmed per person, which promotes the process of degradation of soil fertility. Furthermore, the low productivity and the precarious balance on farms are accompanied by a broad movement of decapitalisation, in order to maintain the labour force.

The neo- communitarian theory reduces the complexity of relationships and relations in underdeveloped societies, especially in African economies, to community constraints, thus excluding from the field of analysis a number of phenomena that have considerable importance in the recent evolution of underdeveloped economies. Despite the major criticisms they apply to the general economic equilibrium school of thought , institutionalist theories do not on the whole offer us a way out of the crisis in development studies. Throughout this section, we have demonstrated their inability to analyse and understand the mutations and evolutions in progress in most Third World countries. The difference between transitions is a particular blind spot for these theories. Beyond a few ad hoc recommendations, these different approaches have not been able to revive reflection on development strategies. The limitations of the neo-institutionalist theory reside in its methodological choices and the option of methodological individualism. While this methodological choice permits a more detailed analysis of the behaviour of economic actors and challenges Walrassian rationality, it does not make it possible to analyse the differentiated transitions and evolutions taking place in underdeveloped countries. These phenomena are structural in nature and therefore require global visions and comprehensive analytical grids.

Section IV

Revival of the Structuralist Approach

The structuralist approach has played an important role in the emergence and development of development economics. This approach took shape in the 1940s and 1950s in Latin America with the work of ECLA and R. Prebisch, in Europe with F. Perroux and G. Myrdal and in the United States with A. Hirschman. This approach differs from the neoclassical approach in that it challenges the equilibrium model and its ability to ensure coherent allocation of productive resources. Influenced by the Keynesian approach, the structuralist approach defends the idea of state intervention in economic regulation and in correcting market imperfections (Oman and Wignaraja 1991).

The most important contribution of structuralist studies, however, resides in their consideration of structural aspects in analysing Third World economies. Thus, underdevelopment is not analysed as a natural phenomenon, but as an historical situation linked to the breakdown of productive structures and to the phenomena of domination exerted by the international economy. According to structuralist analysis, the global economy is made up of two poles with totally different productive structures. Production structures are thus heterogeneous, to the extent that they include low-productivity traditional sectors and high-productivity modern sectors. Productive structures in peripheral areas are specialised in a number of primary products that are exported to developed countries. Contrary to the peripheral areas, productive structures in developed countries are homogeneous, in that all sectors use the same production techniques. Furthermore, these structures are diversified allowing central economies to operate in a coherent manner.

The impact of these structures is central to structural analysis of the phenomena of underdevelopment. According to this approach, structural unemployment in underdeveloped countries is due to the heterogeneous nature of productive structures. On one hand, labour-intensive traditional sectors cannot employ all the manpower generated by rapid population growth. On the other hand, modern sectors use capital-intensive technologies and provide few jobs.

This approach also views foreign deficits as an expression of the productive structures of peripheral countries. While the elasticity of demand for the import of manufactured goods in peripheral areas is higher than one, the elasticity of demand for the import of primary goods in central areas is lower than one. This difference in elasticity is responsible for the chronic trade deficits of peripheral countries. This situation is further aggravated by the tendency of central countries, thanks to technological progress, to substitute synthetic intermediary products for raw materials and primary products imported from peripheral countries. The difference between the elasticities of demand for imports and the limited number of products exported by peripheral countries is responsible for the steady deterioration of the terms of trade. According to the structuralist approach, these phenomena create a natural trend towards uneven development between the two poles of the global economy and perpetuate underdevelopment in the peripheral areas.

With that background in mind, structuralists have formulated a number of recommendations aimed at breaking out of the vicious circle of underdevelopment and initiating new development strategies in the periphery. First of all, they emphasise the role of the state in correcting market imperfections, especially by setting up a new development strategy aimed at the domestic market. In addition, this approach put forward the idea of unbalanced growth and the need to concentrate investment in strategic sectors capable of stimulating the economy as a whole. The strategies suggested by the structuralist approach sought to replace imported consumer goods by local goods. These import-substitution strategies led to a severe regulation of imports, in order to build up the competitiveness of industrial activities developed throughout the periphery.

The structuralist approach that developed following the end of the Second World War combined considerable theoretical reflection with a number of proposed development strategies.

According to this approach, through concentrating development on the domestic market and through state intervention, it should be possible to reverse the trend of uneven development between the centre and the periphery and allow growth to take off in underdeveloped economies.

This approach began to be challenged at the end of the 1960s, however. First, the stagnation of Latin American economies and of all the economies that adopted import-substitution strategies led to criticism of the structuralist approach. This development strategy did not enable the periphery to recover high growth rates and aggravated the external deficits of underdeveloped economies. In addition, at the end of the 1960s, there was the emergence of dependency theories, which criticised the theoretical foundations and the "reforming" political proposals of the structuralist approach. For the dependency theorists, the failure of import-substitution strategies was proof that structuralist recommendations could develop nothing but further underdevelopment and that the development of the periphery required a radical break with the global economy.

This criticism was responsible for the marginalisation of the structuralist approach in the 1970s. The approach was even more strongly criticised in the 1980s, with the return in force in the field of development economics of the pure general equilibrium model and the Washington consensus's attack on all forms of government intervention in the running of developing economies.

The decline of the Washington consensus following the failure of structural adjustment programmes led, however, to a revival of the structuralist approach and to the emergence at the end of the 1980s of a new theoretical model based on that approach. The point of departure for neo-structuralism was a double criticism of the theoretical foundations and the development options of structural adjustment programmes. From a theoretical standpoint, the new approaches criticised the Washington consensus's concentration on supply issues and the marginalisation of demand in the analysis of disequilibrium in underdeveloped countries. Accordingly, they proposed a rehabilitation of demand as a category of analysis and as a foundation for new development policies (Fontaine and Jacmart 1993).

In the early 1980s, advocates of neo-structuralism were already criticising the stabilisation programmes of the World Bank and IMF, which they considered ill-suited to absorbing deficits while maintaining growth in underdeveloped countries (Taylor 1981). The restrictive monetary policy, recommended by the IMF, led to a rapid increase in production costs, which led to a reduction in supply and to renewed social conflicts over distribution. According to the neo- structuralists, this drop in supply and the ensuing inflationary pressures can increase disequilibrium between supply and demand. Furthermore, increased exports are not an inevitable result of devaluation, since they require an elasticity of demand for these exports higher than one. Devaluation does, however, lead to higher prices for imported goods and particularly equipment, which leads to higher production costs and reduced investment. According to the neo-structuralists, the stabilisation advocated by Bretton Woods institutions cannot reduce deficits, but actually increases them and thus perpetuates the dependency of underdeveloped countries.

Neo-structuralists s follow the structuralist approach in attempting to revive demand, while criticising the neo-liberal stabilisation policies inspired by the Walrassian model. They also remind us that development studies should take into consideration the specific structural aspects of underdeveloped societies. They pointed to structural rigidities that prevent the spontaneous balance between supply and demand, and they called for government regulation. These analyses also related to both Marxist and classical analyses, since their models included production costs and analysed inflation as the result of conflicts between salaries and profits.

Neo-structuralist analyses differ from the founders of the structuralist approach in opting for a comparative static analysis of equilibrium situations. In their analyses, the neo- structuralists opt for short-term and medium-term models, including IS/LM models (Taylor 1981). They also differ from the founders on the role of the state. While early structuralist analysis stressed the fundamental role of the state in economic growth dynamics, the new analyses questioned state intervention in the dynamics of accumulation, and recommended firm discipline in the management of public funds, by reducing subsidies on basic commodities and by privatising non-strategic public enterprises. It also considered that to rebuild business competitiveness, it was necessary to reduce customs barriers and to improve the capital content of exports (Romo 1994).

The neo-structuralist approach contains a wide variety of schools and authors. . Looking beyond this diversity, we can distinguish two main approaches. First, there is the Latin American approach, which in keeping with criticism of orthodox stabilisation models, has inspired heterodox stabilisation experiments in Latin America. These models of stabilisation have used administrative control of prices and the suppression of the wage index to fight hyperinflation, especially in Brazil with the Austral Plan and in Argentina with the Cruzado Plan (Grellet 1994; Salama and Valier 1990). However, these experiments failed and were unable to control deficits in those countries and effectively to fight inflation.

A second neo-structuralist approach developed out of the work and early models of L. Taylor. This approach uses a Keynesian perspective to study the impact of various stabilisation scenarios on the economies of underdeveloped countries. This work is theoretical in nature (Ocampo 1987), but also includes applied research on Third World economies, including African economies (Ndulu 1991; Lundahl and Ndulu 1996).

In this section, we present one of L. Taylor's models, in order to discuss the theses of the neo-structuralist approaches, since all the authors draw on his work. L. Taylor, like all neo-structuralist writers, begins by criticising orthodox stabilisation models and questions their ability to fight imbalances in underdeveloped economies while maintaining economic growth. Taylor then emphasises that macroeconomic policies have five objectives (Taylor 1988):

- to maintain a socially acceptable level of growth,

- to maintain a low rate of inflation,

- to increase wealth creation and to improve its distribution,

- to maintain a certain degree of financial and commercial independence with regard to foreign countries,

- to achieve these objectives in a stable environment, capable of overcoming all shocks.

In his study of macroeconomic policies, L. Taylor took particular interest in ways of closing models. He distinguished two methods, a stagnationist system based on stimulating demand and an exhilarationist system based on restructuring supply. This distinction coincides with the traditional distinction between Keynesian underemployment, which corresponds to the stagnationist system, and full employment, which corresponds to the exhilarationist system. In a stagnationist system, increased effective demand and progressive income redistribution leads to increased production and higher rates of utilisation of production capacities, thus increasing employment. On the contrary, in a full employment situation, the economy reacts to a regressive distribution of income, which can increase the share of profits in national income, leading to a revival of investment.

L. Taylor transposes this distinction to underdeveloped economies. He specifies, however, that the two systems can coexist, because of the existence in certain underdeveloped economies of under-utilised resources with rigidity of supply. In that context, IMF stabilisation policies include five types of changes in economic policy (Taylor 1988):

- austerity, in that the public sector must reduce its deficit,

- revision of the rate of exchange in the sense of a devaluation,

- monetary restrictions,

- liberalisation of the market in order to improve macroeconomic performances in the medium term,

- a new regressive policy, with restrictions on salaries and a reduction in the transfer programme.

IMF and World Bank stabilisation policies are supply-side restructuring policies for underdeveloped countries, designed to address macroeconomic imbalances (Fontaine 1993). Supply-side restructuring is not based here on increased investment, but rather on improved and increased production, forming the basis for a recovery in exports. In this framework, control of public spending plays an important role, since it makes possible a decision in favour of foreign demand rather than domestic demand.

The supply-side recovery plan in the orthodox stabilisation model is designed to combat major imbalances, particularly in the balance of payments, while maintaining economic growth. In this schema, supply-side restructuring can lead to a recovery in exports that makes possible an increase in growth and employment. Recovery in domestic demand, owing to increased employment, promotes an increase in the use of productive capacity and an increase in investment. This way, supply-side restructuring can improve major economic balances and bring about recovery in the dynamics of economic growth. However, in his study on a series of stabilisation experiences in the Third World, L. Taylor notes that this schema comes up against some serious obstacles (Taylor 1988). Firstly, elasticity of export supply is low in underdeveloped countries, whereas imports have reached an incompressible level, which makes it difficult to achieve equilibrium in the balance of payments. Furthermore, the orthodox stabilisation model, based on supply-side restructuring and recovery in exports, may be blocked by the impact of export composition, reduced global demand and the protectionist attitudes, which have begun to develop in the global economy.

Export recovery does not necessarily lead to a recovery of growth in domestic markets, however, since devaluation can have recessive effects. Furthermore, monetary restriction and higher interest rates increase production costs and consequently reduce investment. Thus, the recessive nature of orthodox stabilisation programmes can block structural reforms aimed at dynamic integration of underdeveloped economies in the international economy.

L. Taylor systematised his analyses of stabilisation programmes, using different models. In this section, we examine a series of models he developed in 1991 (Taylor 1991). These models are the result of an eclectic mixture of structuralist theories, the Cambridge school and Marxist ideas. The models are based on a series of stylised facts, which the author attempts to clarify. Among these facts, we can cite the following:

- there is a need to identify the power centres in economies and the price rigidity they induce,

- macroeconomic equilibrium does not necessarily lead to full employment of the factors of production. Macroeconomic balance depends on investment, exports, fiscal pressure, etc.,

- the supply of currency is endogenous, and can be adjusted to the level of economic activity and inflation,

- a structuralist conception of inflation based on social conflicts over distribution,

- relations between real and financial sectors may be illustrated by changes in portfolios,

- the import-substitution strategy entails recourse to foreign countries to import capital goods and intermediate goods,

- development is not a harmonious growth process.

In this model, L. Taylor considers a closed economy[3] with a single sector. He specifies two versions in this model: a structuralist version and a neoclassical version. The objective of this model is to determine the evolution of the economy following macroeconomic changes. We will restrict our discussion to a presentation of the structuralist version, which is based on demand.

- **The point of departure of this model is macroeconomic equilibrium**

  (1)   Product = Demand

  (2) $PX = PC + PI + PG$

  $PC + PI + PG - PX = 0$

  where   X: the product

  C: consumption

  I: investment

  G: government spending

  P: prices.

---

[3]   He envisages open economies in other models.

Income distribution can be expressed as follows:

(2) $PX = wbX + rPK$

where   W: monetary wage rate

B: labour share in the product

R: rate of profit

K: capital stock.

Total consumption can be expressed as follows:

(3) $PC = wbX + (1-s)rPK$

workers' savings are equal to zero

capital savings are equal to s.

By combining equation (1), (2) and (3), we obtain the following equation:

(4) $PG + PI - srPK = 0$

This is the equation of macroeconomic balance, which stipulates equality between private saving and government spending.

L. Taylor makes the hypothesis that:

increased capital due to national saving is equal to:

(5) $g^s = sr\ PK/PK$

increased capital linked to investment demand is:

$g^i = PI/PK$

increased government spending linked to increased capital is:

(6) $\mu = PG/PK$

At this level, equation (4) becomes:

(4) $\mu + g^i - g^s = 0$

The investment function in this model is linked to use of production capacity, measured by

(7) $u = X/K.$

u is a contemporary version of the accelerator that makes investment a response to economic activity over the medium term. Investment is also linked to the rate of profit, r, which can be interpreted as businesses' anticipated future receipts or available cash flow when investment is self-financed in periods when credit is rationed.

(8) $g^i = g^i\ (r,u) = g^i\ (p,,u)$

In this model, L. Taylor chose to determine prices using the mark-up principle:

(9) $P = (1 + p)wb = wb/(1 - p)$

which means that prices depend on variable costs (in this example, labour) and a set margin determined by producers.

L. Taylor adds other equations to define his model

(10) $b = L/X$

the ratio of labour to production

(11) $r = [p\ /(1 + p)]u = pu$

In this model, the nominal wage is set by historical conditions, capital stock (K) by expected investment, and government spending (G) by economic policy choices. Prices and profit levels are determined by equation (9). The equations for demand (4), (5) and (8) and the equation for distribution make it possible to determine u and r. The Production comes from equation (7) and the level of use from equation (10). Thus, the model allows L. Taylor to determine the level of employment and production in an economy based on demand. L. Taylor uses the model to examine the consequences and impact of variations in a series of variables (government spending, monetary wages, real wages...) on levels of employment and production (Taylor 1991).

Overall, these models enable L. Taylor to examine the impact of orthodox stabilisation programmes and point out their depressive character in Third World economies. In some cases, these programmes only manage to reduce major imbalances by considerably reducing economic activity. But this deflation does not allow underdeveloped economies to carry out the structural reforms they need for more dynamic integration into the international economy. From this standpoint, the structuralist approach is very interesting, since it makes it possible to grasp the limitations of orthodox approaches to stabilisation.

Despite their interest, the new structuralist models cannot, however, overcome the current crisis in development economics and its inability to analyse and understand the mutations and transformations underway in the Third World. Indeed, owing to their very structure, these models are short-term models and only concern aspects linked to macroeconomic balance. The models cannot and by definition do not seek to understand long-term changes in the Third World. The dynamic transitions that have taken place in Southeast Asian economies, for instance, are the result of strategies and choices operating since the middle of the 1960s and reinforced in the 1970s and 1980s through selective and effective state intervention. Indeed, all Asian governments were characterised by a long-term vision. This vision of the future is even more important during a period of crisis that is marked by deep uncertainty about the future. Their vision enabled the authorities to intervene to favour certain industrial activities over others, in terms of investment, subsidies or institutional support.

Their perception of the future has helped Asian governments to favour strategic sectors over access to financing and credit. On the other hand, economies that did not bother to plan for the future and whose development efforts were limited to managing an agricultural export position inherited from the colonial period, now find themselves on the fringe of the international economy. From that point of view, the changes and transitions facing underdeveloped economies are not the result of short-term macroeconomic choices, but rather the end result of long-term choices and options, which short-term models, such as the neo-structuralist models, can neither understand nor explain.

Furthermore, although they identify themselves with the structuralist tradition, these models have a simplified vision of structures. Their conception of structures stops at an examination of distribution in terms of opposition and conflict between wage earners and profit-makers. This conception, although not without merit, has its limitations, since production is envisaged in the form of macroeconomic sequences, without paying the slightest attention to productive structures. From this standpoint, the neo-structuralist approach does not seem capable of analysing the changes in progress in underdeveloped countries. Indeed, while distribution issues are not marginal to the differentiated transitions experienced by underdeveloped countries, it appears important to study productive structures, in order to understand them. Analysis of the experience of Southeast Asian economies shows that these economies have paid particular attention to productive structures, since, through strong state intervention, they have sought to develop strategic sectors linked to the development of new technologies in order to improve their competitiveness. Furthermore, the Asian experience demonstrates the close and dynamic relationships in industrialisation between industries linked to the domestic market and export industries. The needs of the population should not be neglected, on the pretext of the demands of globalisation and the need to form part of the global market. This process of "walking on two legs" requires particular attention to be given to wages. These should not be viewed merely as a cost to be controlled, but also as a market outlet, whose development determines the future of industries linked to the domestic market. Countries on the fringe of the international economy have paid little attention to the evolution of their productive structures, and after their experience of import-substitution, have opened up their economies and sacrificed their national economic structures in hopes of integrating with the globalisation movement. Despite the importance of the issue of productive structures, the neo- structuralist approach only pays limited attention to it.

Section V

The Cultural Approach

The structural adjustment crisis was behind the development and confirmation of a new approach to development economics. This is the cultural approach, which is found largely in francophone literature. It puts forward the hypothesis that the failure of adjustment is simply a manifestation of the crisis affecting the North's attempts to Westernise the South.

UNESCO's work , which sought to give a cultural dimension to development, was at the source of the cultural approach in the 1970s (Kellerman 1992). This first generation of work was continued by the work of S. Latouche (1986, 1989, 1991) and G. Rist in the late 1980s (Rist 1994, 1996).

The failure of development strategies in the Third World was the point of departure for the cultural appraoch. According to S. Latouche, "Every technique, has proved to be ineffective. Whether it was international specialisation, import-substitution policies, focusing on heavy industries, promoting those industries that would lead to industrialisation, specialisation in export niches - every recipe has failed" (Latouche 1986: 7-8). This failure led advocates of the cultural approach to challenge the very notion of development. According to these authors, development is a belief in the possibility that through globalisation, the Western myth and model can be extended to the entire planet. From this angle, globalisation is an attempt to impose Western social standards on other societies that have their own specific social standards and constructs. G. Rist states that "the problematic of 'development' is inscribed in the depths of the Western imagination. The idea that growth or progress can develop indefinitely is an assertion that radically distinguishes Western culture from all others" (Rist 1996: 389). From this point of view, underdevelopment according to the cultural approach involves "the extraordinary process of deculturation engendered by the West. Deculturation and Westernisation are two facets of the same phenomenon" (Latouche 1986: 14).

This Eurocentric drive to Westernise the planet is not, however, confined to Westerners alone. It has been reproduced by leaders in the South. Indeed, according to G. Rist, "the 'development' paradigm has become a belief shared equally by all nation-state authorities (and thus by all international organisations), nearly all economic technocrats and a great many populations" (Rist 1996: 390).

This criticism of development and Northern expansionist tendencies provides the cultural approach with an opportunity to define the West, which seeks to impose its model of development and its modes of economic and social organisation. Says Latouche, "The West, whose development forms the paradigm, merits description. A geographical space, whose outlines have been more or less definite over the ages, its borders are increasingly ideological in nature. The West was the home of Hellenism, followed by early Christianity, and the triumphant Roman empire, not to mention the Arab-Islamic empire, and its most typical traits can be found between the Mediterranean basin and the shores of the Atlantic" (Latouche 1986:12). This definition of the West is relatively vague to the extent that it covers different political entities and civilisations. But the author defines his conception of the West more clearly, when he indicates that it is the space dominated by "the belief, unheard of in the rest of the cosmos and in other cultures, in cumulative and linear time, that man has a mission totally to dominate nature, and the belief in reason designed to carry out this action" (Latouche 1986: 13).

It becomes clear that what is being referred to is not so much the West itself as the Western concept of modernity, which has affected European societies at all levels since the French revolution. The first of these levels is the philosophical level, where it has instituted the principle of independent reasoning with respect to religion, following from the works of Thomas Aquinas. Western modernity also established the principle of the separation of politics and religion in managing the politics and affairs of the Polity. Finally, this evolution in ideas was accompanied by great scientific and technical progress, which made possible a more rational approach to political and economic structures. This is the heart of the Western model. According to the cultural approach, the function of development is to extend it to the entire planet.

Cultural theorists are opposed to the extension of this model, since they consider that other regions of the world, and the Third World in particular, have their own cultural and social models which should be developed. Cultural writers have an essentialist conception of human societies, to the extent that they consider that every society has a unique culture that forms its world of perceptions and its social imagination. According to these theorists, this cultural universe is stable over time and is not subject to outside influence.

Orientalist studies of the Arab world are an illustration of the essentialist grid of cultural analysts. They consider Arab-Muslim societies to be different from Western societies in terms of the sources of legitimate authority. Indeed, while Western legitimacy is temporal, in Arab-Muslim societies, according to B. Badie, "Only God is right, or more exactly his revelation, which is extended to his prophet. This argument for legitimacy, according to certain traditions, can perhaps benefit the first four caliphs, the family of the prophet or his descendants, particularly in duodecimal Shiism, to the twelfth imam" (Badie 1987). This version of legitimacy has its source in the conception of the original Islam of the Muslim community, the Umma, as a totalising community with a universal vocation. This concept allowed the state of Medina to overcome tribal conflicts and political contests over regional leadership and opened up new horizons for the community. Indeed, the Medina model created by the prophet proposed the "myth of a social order written into divine law" (Camau 1990) as an alternative to the tribal social order. In this order, authority could only belong to God and could only be exercised by an intermediary (the prophet or the Commander of the Faithful), to whom the community must swear obedience. Legitimacy could only be based on respect for religious precepts.

According to Orientalists, in societies where political life is dominated by religion , the ulama, or religious scholars, should hold a central position in legitimising political authorities, since they determine whether or not political leaders respect religious standards. Thus, as M. Camau points out, "allegiance is due to the prince, to the extent that the ulama consider him faithful to the letter of Islamic law" (Camau 1990: 413).

In the view of the Orientalists, this religious legitimacy calls into question all forms of temporal legitimacy in Islamic countries. It compromises any attempt to import elements of Western political modernity. Indeed, in the words of B. Badie, "to the extent that the state provides the means, particularly territorial means, for its sovereignty, it increases its illegitimacy and makes the prince's effort to achieve legitimisation all the more difficult. If it lays claim to a Weberian political monopoly, it deprives itself of the legitimising function of the ulama; if it concedes them this function, it reduces its political effectiveness" (Badie 1987: 21). According to Orientalists, the temporal sphere's obedience to the spiritual sphere in Arab-Muslim societies jeopardises the grafting of

78

elements of Western modernity, and invites these societies to define their own ways of transforming the structures of the exercise of political power.

These analyses have immediate political ramifications in that they devalue the democratic struggle (an avatar of Western political modernity) in Arab societies. Furthermore, according to cultural theorists, the impact of culture leads to specific political behaviour in different societies. The spread and intensification throughout Arab countries of a political practice that draws its inspiration from Islam merely follows the natural course of events. Islam is attempting to revitalise the Medina model and use it as an alternative to the current crisis of the state in the Arab world. According to cultural theorists, who have rediscovered the analyses of political Islam, this crisis is a result of the foreign, imported nature of the reigning political order in Arab societies. According to them, Arab societies must become reconciled with their history and their tradition by a return to and a revival of the model of the Islamic state and the submission of political practice to religious authority.

The spread of the Western model continues to this day, according to cultural theorists, following the crisis of the nation-state, through the myths of globalisation and of integration with the globalisation movement, which are presented as the goal to be achieved by underdeveloped countries. J. P. Peemans points out that this pressure to open up national economies is accompanied by symbolic violence aimed at "presenting either as a natural order or as a universal aspiration, even a universal liberation, what is actually a 'world order' that suits the objectives of a new elite, or rather of the new ruling classes that are in process of being formed" (Peemans 1996).

Since its development, the cultural argument has encountered strong opposition and major criticism. The first criticism concerns its conception of culture as an immutable whole, which underestimates the evolutionary dynamics of cultural practices. J. F. Bayart points out that, "cultural theory persists in considering that a culture is made up of a closed, stable set of perceptions, beliefs or symbols that have a strong 'affinity' with specific opinions, attitudes or behaviours" (Bayart 1996: 46). This substantialist conception of culture, which is similar to the German Romantic concept of Zeitgeist, encloses individuals in imagined cultural universes. This vision does not take into consideration the perpetual movement of change, experienced by the different cultural sets, through complex mechanisms of innovation and borrowing, which cancel out the 'pure' nature of different perceptions of the world. To take the example of Arab-Muslim societies, which are considered in the cultural argument to be an example of societies where the political sphere is subject to the religious sphere, we can observe a slow yet far-reaching evolution in recent decades, with the emergence of the 'secular' person (Hammouda 1995). This person, far from rejecting religion, which continues to be a daily practice, is beginning to allow the principle of separation between politics and religion. Certainly, this principle does not find political expression and is not the result of a revolution violent enough to be noticed; but it is at the heart of an insidious evolution in society.

Acceptance of this principle does not contradict a return to Islam, nor individual attempts to seek refuge from the ideological crisis in Islam. The principle is even fuelled by the return to religion, to the extent that holding religion sacred leads individuals to grant it status as the foundation of self-consciousness and to refuse to associate it with the vagaries of the temporal sphere.

The emergence of this new person in the Arab world comes at the crossroads of three major historical developments. The first of these involves the long, slow trend towards the separation of political and religious authority. This separation began during the Abbasid caliphate with the appearance of an important figure: the Vizier. The Vizier was an official who took care of the administrative management of the empire. By the 9th century, his importance had increased and spread to Andalusia, with the Omeyyad caliphs of Spain and the Fatimids of North Africa. The Vizier, who defined the general orientations of the empire and ensured their implementation, with the approval of the caliph, introduced a new sharing of roles between religious authorities and political authorities. In the words of R. Mantran, "there was a separation between religious authority -the sphere of the caliph- and political authority -the sphere of the vizier" (Mantran 1990). With the weakening of the Muslim empires, political authority increasingly took precedence over religious authority.

This tradition was consolidated under the Ottoman Empire from the fifteenth century. Political authority under the Ottomans was personified by the Sultan, who held absolute power and religious legitimacy. The Sultan appointed a Grand Vizier and senior officials in charge of handling the affairs of the empire. This period also saw the beginning of the distinction between public law and religious law. The Ottoman Empire underwent a series of reforms, the most important of which were the Tanzimat reforms, which led to the promulgation of the constitution in 1876. This movement reached its height in 1924, with the end of the caliphate and the establishment of a secular republic by K. Atatürk.

This secular political practice was reinforced by a twofold evolution in thinking and theory in the Arab world. The first was linked to the Arab Nahda movement, with such thinkers as R. Tahtawi, M. Abdou, J. Al-

Afghani, A. Abderrazik and others. This movement advocated a series of changes aimed at breaking out of dependency and underdevelopment. The most important was the reform of structures for the exercise of political power through separation from the religious sphere. Parallel to the Nahda movement, the rise of mystical movements from the end of the seventeenth century influenced religious practice in the Arab world. These movements, resulting from the influences of hermetic philosophy on Arab thought, stated that while divinity is inaccessible, it is possible to come in contact with its emanations through prayer and rigorous efforts of asceticism and conjuration. In our view, these movements played an important role in the emergence of the secular person, because they made religion a personal issue involving an individual's relationship with the divinity.

Finally, the emergence of the modern school in the Arab world at the end of the nineteenth century led to the devaluing of Koranic schools and the replacement of traditional elite groups, such as the ulama, by modernist elite groups. These elite groups were further encouraged by the construction of the modern state, which ensured their rapid rise. The conjunction of these three factors explains the evolution of beliefs in the Arab world and the emergence of a "secular" person, whom the crisis in the modern state only rarely pushes towards a commitment to Islamic political movements. *This is why, in this day and age, it seems difficult to support the hypothesis that political legitimacy in the Arab world is accompanied by religious legitimacy, which forbids all modernisation of political authority in the direction of enhanced participation by citizens.*

The evolution of the relationship between religion and politics is also indicative of the historical changes and mutations that can affect cultural logic and perceptions. Cultures and perceptions evolve and change by following different types of strategies (Bayart 1996). Among these strategies, we can cite extraversion tactics, essentially linked to colonial presence, transfer practices or authentication procedures. However, openness and the importation of foreign cultural elements are necessarily accompanied by adaptations and reinterpretations of foreign cultural schemas. J. F. Bayart describes "the transfer of meaning from one practice, place or perception, or from one symbol or text to another, because it is, almost by definition, reinterpretation and derivation" (Bayart 1996: 81).

People thus appropriate and reinterpret foreign cultural practices and perceptions. This permanent reinvention of exogenous cultural contributions and their ownership provides a hybrid picture of local cultural identities.

This act of appropriating exogenous contributions is apparent when we examine the specific relationships each culture creates with the economy and with commercial relationships. The development of capitalism in the periphery demonstrates that this form of social organisation can be adjusted to community relationships and traditional solidarity. As J. F. Bayart states, "the projection in time of the capitalist economy on the periphery is hardly a linear process. It combines with specific temporalities, which are generally attached to specific places and historical territories: capitalism is obliged to deal with the active memories of the neighbourhood, the bazaar, the chieftainship, the slum and the country" (Bayart 1994). Indeed, while in Europe and in other countries, capitalism required the dissolution of community relationships and the emergence of individuals who were joined together by commercial relationships, the development of capitalism in the periphery seems to take advantage of traditional forms of solidarity (ethnic communities, regional communities, etc.) and even uses them as the heart and foundation of its development.

It thus follows that, contrary to the claims of the cultural theorists, culture is not a closed and immutable entity; rather it evolves, is transformed and undergoes change in time and space. This evolution is the result of dialogue, borrowing and exchanges between different cultures. These exchanges do not exclude attempts at domination or the wish to exercise hegemony. These dialogues are, however, a source of interbreeding and of mixing between different countries, which means that a "pure civilisation, whose members are organically linked in an indissociable whole, is a pure fiction" (Shayegan 1996).

Because of its basic hypotheses on the immutability and the stability of cultural universes, the cultural approach is unable to analyse and understand the dynamics of the evolution of the Third World. In this evolution, it only concerns itself with the marginalisation of certain regions, such as Africa and the Arab world, which it sees as a demonstration of the failure of the North's attempt to Westernise the South. But what can one say of the experiences of other countries, especially in Asia, where for many years the Confucian cultural universe was presented as incompatible with economic development? How can we explain the development, in a great number of Third World countries, of legal and rational forms of political and economic management, the importation of elements of Western political modernity and the relative success of the transplant? How can we understand the important protest movements against political authoritarianism and the calls for democracy in the Third World in recent years? Are these popular movements a negation of their cultural identities? The cultural approach can provide no answer for these important questions.

The cultural approach also comes up against the fundamental question of alternatives to the development crisis in the periphery. Few cultural theorists are interested in that question. G. Rist proposes three ways of going beyond the current limitations of the different development projects (Rist 1996):

- The first way involves pursuing the growth necessary to satisfy the fundamental needs of the people (Coméliau 1991). However, the authors recommend controlling the structure of growth and directing it towards essential goods.

- The second way is inspired by the practices of certain social movements in the South, which, faced with the failure of development experiences, have opted for the political struggle of marginalised societies. As G. Rist notes, "Despite 'development', the idea is to organise the creation of new ways of life, which lie between modernisation, which brings suffering and yet confers certain advantages, and tradition, which can be a source of inspiration, but which can never be revived" (Rist 1996).

- Finally, the third way is that of radical criticism of the economic vision behind all the presuppositions and concepts that underlie the idea of development.

The alternatives put forward by cultural theorists do not seem to provide ways to create concrete strategies for a different social development. Cultural theorists propose lines for further thought, but no concrete alternatives. G. Rist recognises the difficulty of giving a concrete content to his project (Rist 1996). Indeed, apart from reorienting the structures and contents of growth, the other proposals of the cultural theorists remain vague and ill defined. The suggestion to reorient growth is not, indeed, completely new, since following the failure of import-substitution strategies in the late 1960s, a number of writers emphasised the importance of giving a new content to economic growth in the South. More specifically, this work considers that development of the domestic market, by enabling a larger share of the population to satisfy its basic needs, could initiate new dynamics of accumulation and growth in the South, and decrease its dependency on international markets. From this standpoint, the cultural approach, which seeks to make a radical break with 'development', merely repeats the traditional proposals of development theory.

Conclusion

The failure of adjustment programmes was the theoretical starting point for the movement criticising the Washington consensus. The questioning of the general equilibrium in the analysis of problems of underdevelopment was inspired by the continuing changes in the field of economic theory and the emergence of new contributions that sought to increase the relevancy of the Walrassian model by modifying some of its basic hypotheses. Questioning the Washington consensus and changes in the field of political economy were the source of the new theoretical conceptions in development economics, which we refer to as post-adjustment development economics. In this paper, we have sought to carry out a critical examination of the different approaches that dominate the field of study of development problems. We have distinguished four different approaches. First, an approach closely related to endogenous growth theories, which attempts to revise development theory by returning to the founding fathers. The second approach, institutionalism, is particularly concerned with market imperfections and studies the role and impact of institutions in the regulation and operation of underdeveloped economies. The third or post-Keynesian approach starts from its criticism of the orthodox foundations of models of stabilisation, and attempts to construct new strategies designed to stimulate internal demand. Finally, the cultural approach considers the failure of development strategies to be above all the failure of the North's attempts to Westernise the world following independence.

Our critical examination of the different approaches to post-adjustment development economics has demonstrated their inability to grasp and explain the mutations and evolutions in progress in the Third World. These limitations require a renovation of development theories and the construction of approaches capable of analysing the current dynamics in most underdeveloped countries, and looking beyond the specific features of each individual economy to the general transitions experienced by Third-World economies. This would require economists to take a particular interest in the study of the articulation of concrete modes of accumulation and regulation procedures that make it possible to manage imbalances and to keep tensions at tolerable levels.

Bibliography

Abraham-Frois, G., 1993, *Keynes et la macroéconomie contemporaine*, Economica, 4e édition.

Akerlof, A. G., 1970, 'The Market for "Lemons": Quality, Uncertainty and the Market Mechanism', *Quarterly Journal of Economics*, Vol. LXXXIV, No. 3, August 1970.

Akerlof, A. G. and Yellen, J. L., 1985, 'A Near-rational of the Business Cycle, with Wage and Price Inertia', *Quarterly Journal of Economics*, supplement, 100 (5).

Alchian, A. A. and Demsetz, H., 1972, 'Production, Information Costs and Economic Organisation', *American Economic Review,* Vol. 62.

Amable, B. and Guellec, D., 1992, "Les théories de la croissance endogène", *Revue d'économie politique*, No. 102, Mai-juin.

Amin, S., 1979, *Classe et nation dans l'histoire et la crise contemporaine*, Les éditions de minuit, Paris.

Amin, S., 1991, *L'empire du chaos*, Paris, L'Harmattan.

Amin, S., 1996, *Les défis de la mondialisation*, Paris, L'Harmattan.

Antonelli, G. and Raimondo, L., 1992, "Quelques unes des contributions les plus récentes au débat théorique sur l'économie du développement", *Economie rurale*, No. 212, novembre/décembre.

Arrow, K. J., 1974, *Les limites de l'organisation*, PUF.

Artus, P., 1993, "Croissance endogène : revue des modèles et tenatives de synthèse", *Revue économique*, No. 2, mars.

Badie, B., 1987, "Etat et légitimité en monde musulman : crise de l'universalité et crise des concepts", *Annuaire de l'Afrique du Nord*, Editions du CNRS.

Balassa, B., 1971, *The Structure of Protection in Developing Countries,* Johns Hopkins University Press, Baltimore.

Bardhan, P., 1989, 'The New Institutional Economics and Development Theory: A Brief Critical Assessment', *World Development*, Vol. 17, No. 9.

Bardhan, P., 1993, 'Economics of Development and the Development of Economics', *Journal of Economic Perspectives*, Vol. 7, No. 2.

Bardhan, P., 1993, *'Alternative Approaches to Development Economics'*, H. Chenery and T. N. Srinivisan (editors).

Barro, R. J. and 'Sala-I-Martin, X., 1992,Public Finance in Models of Economic Growth', *Review of Economic Studies*, No. 59.

Barro, R. J. and Lee, J. W., 1994, 'Losers and Winners in Economic Growth', *Proceedings of the World Bank* Annual Conference on Development Economics 1993, Washington.

Barro, R. J., 1990, 'Government Spending in a Simple Model of Endogenous Growth', *Journal of Political Economy*, October.

Barro, R. J., 1991, 'Economic Growth in a Cross Section of Countries', *Quarterly Journal of Economics,* May.

Basu, K., 1984, *The Less Developed Economy: A Critique of Contemporary Theory*, Basil Blackwell, Oxford.

Baumol, W. J. and Lee, K. S., 1991, 'Contestable Markets, Trade and Development', *World Bank Research Observer,* Vol. 6, No. 1.

Baumol, W.J., Panzar, J.C., and Willig, R.D. 1988, *Contestable Markets and the Theory of Industry Structure,* H.B. Jovanovich, San Diego.

Bayart, J. F., 1994, "L'invention paradoxale de la modernité économique", in J. F. Bayart, *La réinvention du capitalisme*, Paris, Karthala, p. 18.

Bayart, J. F., 1996, *L'illusion identitaire,* Paris, Fayard, p. 46.

Becker, G., Murphy, K. M. and Tamura, R., 1990, 'Human Capital, Fertility and Economic Growth', *Journal of Political Economy,* Volume 98, October.

Belloc, B., 1987, "Quelques aspects normatifs du problème d'Akerlof", *Revue économique*, No. 1, janvier.

Ben Hammouda, H., 1993, "Développement des rapports marchands et prélèvements : une hypothèse explicative de la crise du mode d'accumulation au Burundi", *Mondes en développement,* Tome 21, No. 82.

Ben Hammouda, H., 1995, *Burundi : Histoire politique et économique d'un conflit*, L'Harmattan.

Ben Hammouda, H., 1995, *Crise, ajustement et atomisation sociale dans le monde arabe,* in S. Amin, H. Ben Hammouda and B. Founou, *Afrique et monde arabe, échec de l'insertion internationale*, Paris, L'Harmattan.

Ben Hammouda, H., 1997, *Les pensées uniques en économie*, Paris, L'Harmattan.

Bently, M. and Oberhofer, T., 1981, 'Property Rights and Economic Development', *Review of Social Economy*, No. 39.

Berthélemy, J. C., Devezeaux de Lavergne, J.-G., Gagey, F., 1991, "L'économie du développement : présentation générale", *Economie et prévision*, No. 97, p. I.

Bhagwati, J. N., 1978, *Anatomy and Consequences of Trade Control Regimes*, NBER, New York.

Binswager, H. and Rosenzweig, M., 1984 (editors), *Contractual Arrangements, Employment and Wages in Rural Labour Markets in Asia*, New Haven, Yale University Press.

Blinder, A., 1979, *Economic Policy and the Great Stagflation*, Academic Press, New York.

Brander, J. A. and Spencer, B., 1985, 'Export Subsidies and International Market Share Rivalry', *Journal of International Economics*, No. 18.

Brander, J. A., 1981, 'Intra-industry Trade in Identical Commodities', *Journal of International Economics*, No. 11.

Brander, J. A. and Krugman, P., 1983, 'A "Reciprocal Dumping" Model of International Trade', *Journal of International Economics*, No. 13.

Brousseau, E., 1993, 'Les théories des contrats : une revue', *Revue d'économie politique*, No. 103, janvier-février.

Cahuc, P. 1993, *Le marché, loi du monde moderne*, Sciences Humaines, Hors-série No. 3, novembre-décembre.

Camau, M., 1990, *Le Maghreb, Collectif, Les régimes politiques arabes*, Paris, PUF.

Carlton, D., 1986, *The Rigidity of Prices, American Economic Review*, Vol. 76.

Chang, H. J., 1993, *The Political Economy of Industrial Policy*, St. Martin's Press, New York.

Cheng, T., Haggard, S. and Kang, D., 1996, *Institutions, Economic Policy and Growth in the Republic of Korea and Taiwan Province of China*, UNCTAD, Geneva, February.

Coase, R., 1987, 'The Nature of the Firm', *Economica*, Vol. NS4; translated into the French as, 'La nature de la firme', *Revue française d'économie*, 1987.

Cochet, H., 1996, *Burundi : la paysannerie dans la tourmente. Eléments d'analyse sur les origines du conflit politico-ethnique*, Fondation Charles Léopold Mayer pour le progrès de l'Homme, Paris.

Coméliau, C., 1991, "Les relations Nord-Sud", *La découverte*, Paris.

Datta-Chadhuri, M., 1990, 'Market Failure and Government Failure', *Journal of Economic Perspectives*, Vol. 4, No. 3.

Dupuy, J. P., Eymard-Duvernay, F., Favereau, O., Orléan, A., Salais, R., and Thévenot, L., 1989, "Introduction", *Revue économique*, Vol. 40, No. 2, mars.

Dutraive, V., 1993, "La firme entre transaction et contrat : Williamson épigone ou dissident de la pensée institutionnaliste?", *Revue d'économie politique*, Vol. 103, No. 1, janvier-février.

Economie appliquée, 1990, "Approches des institutions économiques", Vol. 43, No. 3.

Eswaran, M. and Kotwal, A., 1985, 'A Theory of Two-tier Labour Markets in Agrarian Economics', *American Economic Review*, March.

Fall, Babacar, 1997, (ed.), *Ajustement structurel et emploi au Sénégal*, Dakar, CODESRIA.

Favereau, O., 1989, "Marchés internes, marchés externes", *Revue économique,* No. 2, mars.

Favereau, O., 1995, *Développement et économie des conventions*, Ph. Hugon, G, Pourcet and S. Quiers-Valette, op. cit.

Feeny, D., 1979, 'Competing Hypothesis of Underdevelopment: A Thai Case Study', *The Journal of Economic History*, No. 39.

Fontaine, J. M. and Jacmart, M. C., 1993, "La réhabilitation de la demande. Points de repères et analyses appliquées", *Tiers-Monde*, Tome XXXIV, No. 135, juillet-septembre.

Fontaine, J. M., 1993, "Demande et investissement dans le processus d'ajustement", *Tiers-Monde*, Tome XXXIV, No. 135, juillet-septembre.

Gillis, X., 1987, "La nature de la firme et la théorie des coûts de transaction", *Revue française d'économie*, Vol. II, No. 1.

Gordon, R. J., 1990, 'What is New Keynesian Economics?', *Journal of Economic Literature*, No. 28, September.

Greenaway, D., 1987, 'The New Theories of Intra-industry Trade', *Bulletin of Economic Research*, April.

Grellet, G., 1994, *Les politiques économiques des pays du Sud*, IEDES/PUF.

Guerrien, B., 1990, "Quelques réflexions sur institutions, organisations et histoire", *Economie appliquée*, Tome XLIII, No. 3.

Guillaumont, P., 1992, "Déclin et renouveau de l'économie du développement", *Revue française d'économie*, Vol. X, No. 1, hiver 1995.

Haggard, S., 1990, *Pathways from the Periphery: The Politics of Growth in the Newly Industrialising Countries,* Cornell University Press, Ithaca.

Hellier, J., 1993, "La similitude dans l'échange international : une revue critique des approches théoriques", *Revue française d'économie*, Vol. VIII, No. 1, hiver 1993.

Helpman, E. and Razin, A., 1991, (eds.), *International Trade and Trade Policy*, The MIT Press.

Henin, P. Y. and Ralle, P., 1994, "Les nouvelles théories de la croissance. Quelques apports pour la politique économique", *Revue économique*, Volume 44, Hors-Série.

Hirschman, A., 1964, "La stratégie du développement économique", *Editions ouvrières*, Paris.

Hugon, Ph., 1995, "Robinson ou vendredi? La rationalité économique en Afrique", *Sciences humaines*, No. 47, février, p. 11.

Hymer, S., 1976, *The International Operations of National Firms: A Study of Direct Foreign Investment*, MIT Press.

Katz, L., 1986, 'Efficiency Wage Theories: A Partial Evaluation', *NBER Macroeconomics Annual*.

Kellerman, L., 1992, *La dimension culturelle du développement*, Paris, L'Harmattan/UNESCO.

Krueger, A. O. and Summers, L. H. 1988, 'Efficiency Wages and the Inter-Industry Wage Structure', *Economica*, Vol. 56.

Krueger, A. O., 1978, *Liberalisation Attempts and Consequences*, NBER, New York.

Krugman, P. R., 1981, 'Trade, Accumulation and Uneven Development', *Journal of Development Economics*, No. 8.

Krugman, P. R., 1990, *Rethinking International Trade*, The MIT Press.

Krugman, P. R., 1993, 'The Narrow and Broad Arguments for Free Trade, *The American Economic Review*, No. 2, May.

Krugman, P. R., 1993, 'Toward a Counter-counter-revolution in Development Theory', *Proceedings of the World Bank Annual Conference on Development Economics 1992*, Washington.

Krugman, P., 1994, 'The Myth of Asia's Miracle', Foreign Affairs, November/December.

Krugman, P., 1995, *Development, Geography and Economic Theory*, MIT Press, Cambridge and London.

95

Laffont, J. J., 1987, "Le risque moral dans la relation de mandat", *Revue économique*, No. 1, janvier.

Latouche, S., 1986, *Faut-il refuser le développement?*, Paris, PUF.

Latouche, S., 1989, *L'occidentalisation du monde*, Paris, La découverte.

Latouche, S., 1991, *La planète des naufragés, essai sur l'après-développement*, Paris, La découverte.

Little, I. M. D., Scitovsky, T. and Scott, M. F. G. 1970, *Industry and Trade in Some Developing Countries*, Oxford University Press, London.

Lordon, F., 1991, "La redécouverte des rendements croissants", *Observations et diagnostics économiques*, No. 37, juillet.

Lucas, R. E. (Jr.), 1990, 'Why Doesn't Capital Flow from Rich to Poor Countries', *American Economic Review*, Vol. 80, No. 2, May.

Lucas, R., 1988, 'On the Mechanics of Economic Development', *Journal of Monetary Economics*, No. 22.

Lundahl, M. and Ndulu, B. J., 1996, *New Directions in Development Economics. Growth, Environmental Concerns and Government in the 1990s*, London, Routledge.

Mahieu, F. R., 1990, *Les fondements de la crise économique en Afrique*, L'Harmattan, p. 9.

Mahieu, F. R., 1995, "Les stratégies individuelles face à la pauvreté : Côte d'Ivoire versus Burundi", Ph. Hugon, G. Pourcet and S. Quiers-Valette (editors), *L'Afrique des incertitudes*, Paris, IEDES/ PUF, p. 119.

Mankiw, N. G., 1985, 'Small Menu Costs and Large Business Cycle: A Macroeconomic Model', *Quarterly Journal of Economics*, 100 (2), May.

Mantran, R., 1990, "Dynamique politique: l'évolution historique", Collectif, *Les régimes politiques arabes*, op. cit., p. 48.

Michaely, M., 1977, 'Exports and Growth: An Empirical Investigation', *Journal of Development Economics*, Vol. 4.

Mkandawire, Thandika and Olukoshi, Adebayo, 1995, *Between Liberalisation and Oppression: The Politics of Structural Adjustment in Africa*, Dakar, CODESRIA.

Myrdal, G., 1957, *Rich Land and Poor,* Harper, New York.

Nabli, M. K. and J. B. Nugent, 1989, 'The New Institutional Economics and Its Applicability to Development', *World Development*, Vol. 17, No. 9.

Ndulu, B. J., 1991, Growth and Adjustment in Sub-Saharan Africa, A. Chiber and S. Fischer (editors), *Economic Reform in Sub-Saharan Africa*, World Bank, Washington.

North, D. C., 1994, 'The New Institutional Economics and Development', *Forum,* No. 2, Vol. 1, May.

North, D., 1988, 'Institutions and Economic Growth: An Historical Introduction', *World Development*, Vol. 17, No. 9.

North, D., 1990, *Institutions, Institutional Change and Economic Performance*, Cambridge University Press.

North, D. and Thomas, R., 1973, *The Rise of the Western World. A New Economic History*, Cambridge University Press.

Ocampo, J. A., 1987, 'The Macroeconomic Effect of Import Controls. A Keynesian Analysis', *Journal of Development Economics*, No. 27.

Okun, A. M., 1981, 'Prices and Quantities: A Macroeconomic Analysis', *The Brookings Institution,* Washington.

Oman, Ch. P. and Wignaraja, G., 1991, *L'évolution de la pensée économique sur le développement depuis 1945,* Centre de développement, Paris, OCDE.

Orléan, A., 1989, "Pour une approche cognitive des conventions économiques", *Revue économique,* Vol. 40, No. 2, mars.

Orléan, A., 1991, "Logique walrassienne et incertitude qualitative : des travaux d'Akerlof et Stiglitz aux conventions de qualité", *Economies et sociétés, série Economia,* PE, No. 14, janvier.

Orléan, A., 1994, "Vers un modèle général de la coordination économique par les conventions", in Orléan (ed.), *Analyse économique des conventions,* Paris, PUF, p. 13.

P. Rosenstein-Rodan, P., 1943, 'Industrialisation of Eastern and South Eastern Europe', *Economic Journal,* Vol. 53.

Peemans, J. P., 1996, "L'utopie globalitaire", *Nouveaux cahiers de l'IUED,* No. 5, PUF.

Rist, G., 1994, (ed.), *La culture otage du développement?,* Paris, L'Harmattan/EADI.

Rist, G., 1996, *Le développement, histoire d'une croyance occidentale,* Paris, Presses de Sciences politiques.

Romer, P., 1993, 'The New Keynesian Synthesis', *The Journal of Economic Perspectives,* Vol. 7, No. 1, Winter.

Romer, P., 1986, 'Increasing Returns and Long-run Growth', *Journal of Political Economy,* No. 94.

Romer, P., 1990, 'Endogenous Technological Change', *Journal of Political Economy.*

Romer, P., 1993, 'Two Strategies for Economic Development: Using Ideas and Producing Ideas', *Proceedings of the World Bank Annual*

Conference on Development Economics 1992, Washington.

Romo, H. G., 1994, "De la pensée de la CEPAL au néo-libéralisme, du néo-libéralisme au néo-structuralisme, une revue de la littérature sud-américaine", *Tiers-Monde*, No. 140, octobre-décembre.

Rosenstein Rodan, P. 1961, Notes on the 'Theory of the Big Push', H. S. Ellis and H. Wallich (eds.), *Economic Development for Latin America*, St. Martin's Press, New York.

Ruttan, W. and Hayami, Y., 1984, 'Toward a Theory of Induced Institutional Innovation', *Journal of Development Studies*, No. 20.

Salais, R., 1989, "L'analyse économique des conventions du travail", *Revue économique*, Vol. 40, No. 2, mars.

Salama, P. and Valier, J., 1990, *L'économie gangrénée*, La découverte, Paris.

Savvides, A., 1995, 'Economic Growth in Africa', *World Development*, Vol. 23, No. 3.

Shayegan, D., 1996, "Le choc des civilisations", *Esprit*, No. 4, avril, p. 41.

Solow, R. 1956, A Contribution to the Theory of Economic Growth, *Quarterly Journal of Economics*, No. 70, February.

Stiglitz, J. E. and Uy, M., 1996, 'Financial Markets, Public Policy and the East Asian Miracle', *The World Bank Research Observer,* Vol. 11, No. 2, August.

Stiglitz, J. E., 1985, 'Economics of Information and the Theory of Economic Development', *Revista de econometrica*, No. 1.

Stiglitz, J. E., 1986, 'The New Development Economics', *World Development*, Vol. 14, No. 2.

Stiglitz, J. E., 1987, 'The Causes and Consequences of the Dependence of Quality on Price', *Journal of Economic Literature*, Vol. XXV, March.

Stiglitz, J. E., 1988, 'Economic Organisation, Information and Development", H. Chenery and T. N. Srinivasan (editors), *Handbook of Development Economics*, Vol. 1, Elsevier Science Publishers, Amsterdam.

Stiglitz, J. E., 1994, 'The Role of the State in Financial Markets', *Proceedings of the World Bank Annual Conference on Development Economics 1993*, Washington.

Stiglitz, J. E., 1996, 'Some Lessons from the East Asian Miracle', *The World Bank Research Observer*, Vol. 11, No. 2, August.

Stiglitz, J. E., 1997, 'The Role of the Government in Economic Development', M. Bruno and B. Pleskovic (editors), *Annual World Bank Conference on Development Economics 1996*, The World Bank, Washington.

Taylor, J. B., 1980, 'Aggregate Dynamics and Staggered Contracts', *Journal of Political Economy,* Vol. 88.

Taylor, L., 1981, 'IS/LM in the Topics: Diagrammatis of the New Structuralist Macro Critique', W. R. Cline and S. Weintraub (eds.), *Economic Stabilisation in Developing Countries,* The Brookings Institution, Washington.

Taylor, L., 1988, *Varieties of Stabilization Experience. Towards Sensible Macroeconomics in the Third World*, Oxford, WIDER/Clarendon Press.

Taylor, L., 1991, 'Distribution, Inflation and Growth. Lectures on Structuralist Macroeconomic Theory', The MIT Press, Cambridge, Massachusetts.

Toye, J., 1987, "Théorie et expérience du développement. Questions pour le futur", L. Emmerji (editor), *Les politiques de développement et la crise des années 80,* Paris, OCDE.

Tshibaka, Tshikala, 1998, (ed.), *Structural Adjustment and Agriculture in West Africa,* Dakar, CODESRIA.

Villé, Ph. De, 1990, Comportements concurrentiels et équilibre général : de la nécessité des institutions, *Economie appliquée,* No. 3.

Williamson, O. E., 1985, 'The Economic Institutions of Capitalism', *The Free Press*, New York.

Williamson, O.E., 1975, *Markets and Hierarchies: Analysis and Antitrust Implications,* The Free Press, New York.

Yong, H., 1994, "Economie néo-institutionelle et développement. Une analyse synthétique," *Revue d'économie du développement,* No.4.

www.ingramcontent.com/pod-product-compliance
Lightning Source LLC
Chambersburg PA
CBHW061834220326
41599CB00027B/5278